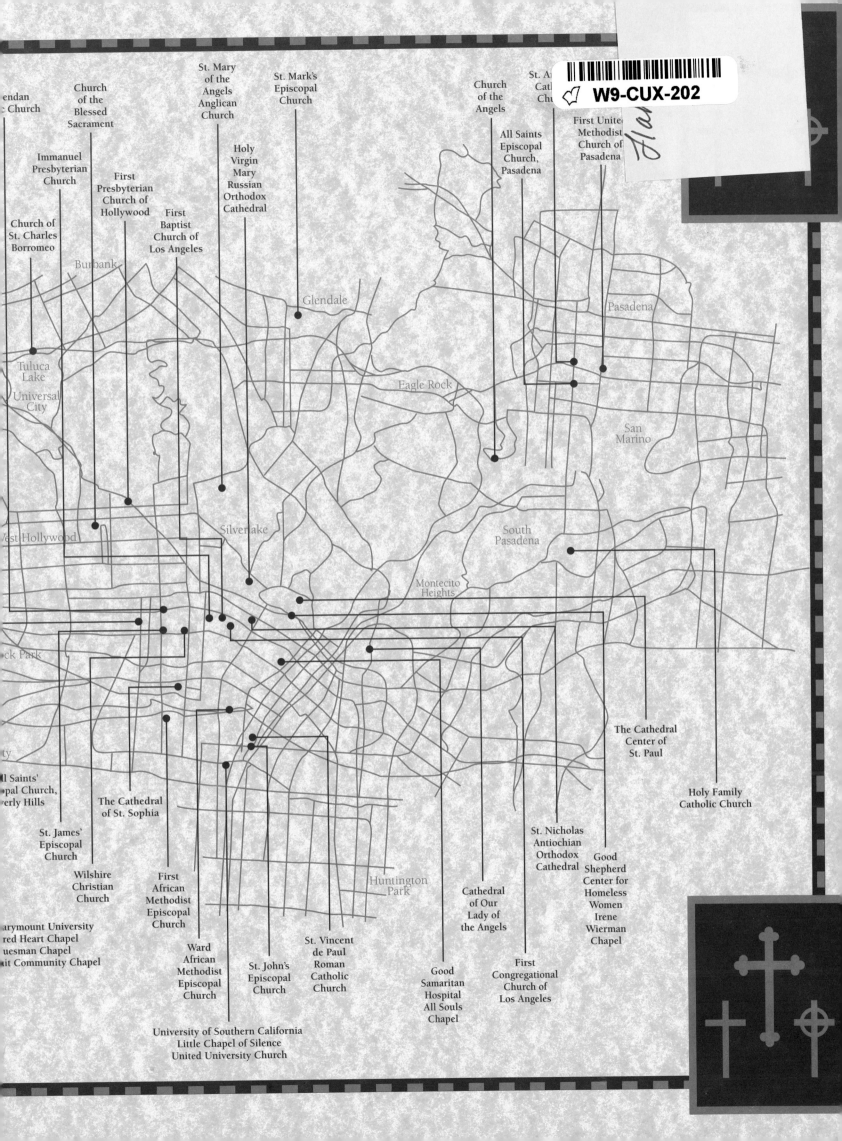

endan
c Church

Church of the
Blessed
Sacrament

St. Mary
of the
Angels
Anglican
Church

St. Mark's
Episcopal
Church

Church
of the
Angels

St. A
Cath
Chu

Immanuel
Presbyterian
Church

First
Presbyterian
Church of
Hollywood

First
Baptist
Church of
Los Angeles

Holy
Virgin
Mary
Russian
Orthodox
Cathedral

All Saints
Episcopal
Church,
Pasadena

First United
Methodist
Church of
Pasadena

Church of
St. Charles
Borromeo

Burbank

Glendale

Pasadena

Tuluca
Lake

Universal
City

Eagle Rock

San
Marino

West Hollywood

Silverlake

South
Pasadena

Montecito
Heights

ck Park

The Cathedral
Center of
St. Paul

Holy Family
Catholic Church

ll Saints'
opal Church,
erly Hills

The Cathedral
of St. Sophia

St. James'
Episcopal
Church

St. Nicholas
Antiochian
Orthodox
Cathedral

Good
Shepherd
Center for
Homeless
Women
Irene
Wierman
Chapel

Wilshire
Christian
Church

First
African
Methodist
Episcopal
Church

Huntington
Park

Cathedral
of Our
Lady of
the Angels

arymount University
red Heart Chapel
uesman Chapel
uit Community Chapel

Ward
African
Methodist
Episcopal
Church

St. John's
Episcopal
Church

St. Vincent
de Paul
Roman
Catholic
Church

Good
Samaritan
Hospital
All Souls
Chapel

First
Congregational
Church of
Los Angeles

University of Southern California
Little Chapel of Silence
United University Church

Jewels in Our Crown®
Churches of Los Angeles

BY CAROLYN LUDWIG

PHOTOGRAPHS BY BRIANNE SANADA

TEXT BY SYDNEY SWIRE

All the best
Carolyn Ludwig

Brianne Sanada

Ludwig Publishing, Incorporated

Los Angeles, California

Copyright © 2003 Carolyn Ludwig

Published 2003 by LUDWIG PUBLISHING, INC.,
Los Angeles, California

Designed by MORRIS JACKSON, San Francisco, California

Library of Congress Control Number: 2003096897

ISBN 0-9744816-0-2 Hardbound
ISBN 0-9744816-1-0 Softbound

First Printing

Printed in Los Angeles by Paper Chase Printing, Inc.

Dedicated with love to
Sister Julia Mary Farley, my friend and mentor.

TABLE OF CONTENTS

INTRODUCTION

Inspiration for this book came to me through life's journeys, some of which were travels to other countries, but most of all because of tugs on my heart by The Holy Spirit. Within each of these churches, one can feel the living history not only of the development of Los Angeles, but of those who sacrificed to build and those who now sacrifice to maintain these magnificent houses of worship. Through this publication we honor those very people who followed their hearts and left us these gifts.

As you read this book and gaze at the awe-inspiring photos I hope that you too will sense The Holy Spirit who dwells in these *Jewels in Our Crown*.

Carolyn Ludwig

Jewels in Our Crown®
Churches of Los Angeles

ALL SAINTS' EPISCOPAL CHURCH

All Saints' Episcopal Church, Beverly Hills

The bell outside the west door

RIGHT: **An angelic candlestick**

OPPOSITE PAGE: **Detail of the pulpit**

The game room of the Beverly Hills Hotel was the unlikely site of the first worship services of what would eventually become All Saints' Parish in Beverly Hills. By 1922, the congregation had raised $26,000 to buy three lots on Santa Monica Boulevard and Camden Drive on which to build a church. The Spanish Colonial Revival-style building was designed by the architectural firm of Johnson Kaufman and Coate; the first services were first held on Easter, 1925.

Nearly 30 years later, when the growth of the membership required a larger church and parish facilities, Roland E. Coate, a principle in the firm which had designed the original

church, was retained to draw plans for the new buildings. He continued the Spanish Colonial Revival theme for the church, and the original structure became the chapel. Again, Easter was the date of the first service in the new church when it opened in 1952.

The church's iron work was executed by Walter Kristensen, and the window above the west door was designed by artist Albert Stewart. The stained glass windows for All Saints', illustrating Biblical scenes as well as individual saints and prophets, were created by the English firms of James Powell and Sons Ltd., Reynolds, Francis and Rohnstock, and Charles Connick and Associates. In the Memorial Chapel, dedicated to members of the parish who died in World War II, the windows include stained glass portraits of St. Elizabeth, St. Anne, St. Eunice and the Virgin Mary.

Its Beverly Hills location naturally attracted actors and entertainment industry professionals. Among the members of the All Saints' congregation were Fred Astaire, Van Johnson, Randolph Scott, George Stevens, Dorothy Lamour, Harold Lloyd and Humphrey Bogart. Many of these stars performed in the church's annual fundraiser, the All Star Revue, which benefited the Episcopal Diocese of Los Angeles.

Johnson Fain Partners architectural firm headed the 1995 renovation of All Saints'. In 1997, parishioner David Davis oversaw the painting of the fresco in the church's apse, and designed the cross which hangs over the altar screen. It is severe on the side turned toward the Sanctuary during Lent, and ornate on the other, which is in use during the rest of the year.

Stonework angels
in the original baptistery
above the font

Windows in the Memorial Chapel,
honoring All Saints' members who
died in World War II

OPPOSITE PAGE: Parishioner David
Davis designed the apse fresco and
the cross on the choir screen in the
Sanctuary

A view of the carved
wooden pulpit

The chapel altar

A detail of the chapel tabernacle

A lunette window illumines the chapel

OPPOSITE PAGE: The original church, built in 1925, is now used as a chapel

Wrought iron lantern

MY SPIRIT HATH

MY

REJOICED IN GOD

SOUL DOGH MAGNIFYthe

LORD

MY SAVIOUR

FOR WITH GOD NOTHING SHALL BE IMPOSSIBLE

HIS NAME IS JOHN

TO THE GLORY OF GOD IN LOVING MEMORY OF DOROTHY PRIMROSE

The Memorial Chapel

OPPOSITE PAGE: Windows celebrating women saints in the Memorial Chapel

Book of Remembrance honors deceased All Saints' Church members

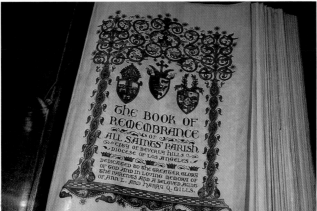

A carved seat in the Memorial Chapel

The triptych next to the altar

ALL SAINTS EPISCOPAL CHURCH

All Saints Episcopal Church, Pasadena

RIGHT: The baptismal font

OPPOSITE PAGE: "The Good Shepherd" by Tiffany Studios

Shields of the Episcopal Church

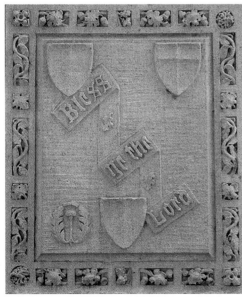

With its stained glass windows designed by Tiffany and Judson Studios, floor tile by Ernest Batchelder, and ornately carved oak woodwork, All Saints is a celebration of the Arts and Crafts Movement of decorative arts particularly popular in California during the early 20th century.

This first Episcopal parish in Pasadena was officially founded in 1886. Its members had met in private homes before purchasing land in 1885 and constructing a wooden church at the corner of Garfield Avenue and Colorado Boulevard. In 1889 the congregation built a church at 132 N. Euclid Avenue.

The architectural firm of Johnson Kaufmann and Coate was selected to design a new building at the Euclid Avenue site in 1923. Its principal Reginald Johnson was the son of the first Episcopal Bishop of Los Angeles. For All Saints, Johnson designed a Gothic Revival-style church built of stone quarried from nearby Bouquet Canyon with a roof of Vermont slate.

Two stained glass windows designed by Tiffany were retained from the 1889 church and installed in the north and south transepts of the new All Saints. The north window represents the Resurrection Angel, and the window in the south transept is the Good Shepherd. Judson Studios, of Southern California, created matching stained glass side panels for both transept windows. From Tiffany also came the choir clerestory windows. The rest of the stained glass throughout the church is in the Arts and Crafts style designed by Judson Studios. Among the subjects for the windows are scenes from the life of Jesus, as well as such biblical figures as Samuel and Eli, St. Thomas, David, Dorcas, and Ruth and Naomi. The inclusion of such a range of women as subjects for stained glass artistry is notable, and other women represented include St. Perpetua and St. Felicitas.

More stained glass illumines the Webb Memorial Chapel. The subjects of its three windows are The Annunciation, Christ at Bethany, and The Resurrection. The altar is framed by a Gothic arch, and four Gothic trusses support the chapel ceiling.

Woodwork throughout All Saints is oak, with carved thistles, pomegranates and acorns symbolizing resurrection and renewal. The carvings of the lectern and pulpit are by the American Seating Company.

Christ is recognized as the Son of God

"The Resurrection Angel" by Tiffany Studios

Traditional Gothic tracery
surrounds the windows

The clerestory
windows were
created by
Judson Studios

"Christ Blessing the Children" was fabricated of Tiffany glass by Judson Studios.

The pulpit carvings are by American Seating Company

The chancel window is dedicated to the love of children

The beams and trusses of the nave resemble those of a ship turned upside down

Gothic-style woodwork in the Webb
Memorial Chapel

OPPOSITE PAGE: The church stone was
quarried from Bouquet Canyon

The carved wooden reredos
in the chapel

The chapel's chandelier
features a cross and crown

CATHEDRAL OF OUR LADY OF THE ANGELS

Cathedral of Our Lady of the Angels,
Los Angeles

RIGHT: A lion
sculpture in
the Children's
Garden

OPPOSITE PAGE: Robert
Graham's sculpture of
Our Lady of the Angels is
above the main entrance

The 38-bell carillon along
Temple Street

The Great Bronze Doors
show culturally diverse
concepts of Mary

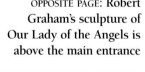

which was dedicated in 1876, had been discussed for years, it wasn't until the Northridge earthquake of 1994 inflicted such seismic damage to the church that Cardinal Roger Mahony began the search for a new site for a new cathedral. Our Lady of the Angels was dedicated in September 2002 after four years of construction.

The main entrance to the cathedral is through the 25-ton, 30-foot tall Great Bronze Doors sculpted by Robert Graham with religious symbols from numerous cultures in high relief. The doors are surmounted by Graham's eight-foot sculpture of Mary, whose face is an amalgam of diverse cultures, and whose halo is formed by natural light.

Moneo chose translucent alabaster for the windows of the cathedral, including the enormous cross-shaped one above the altar, which symbolizes Christ as the light of the world. The side walls are lined by 25 tapestries by artist John Nava. These depict the Communion of Saints, 133 apostles, martyrs, saints and other significant figures in the history of the church. Seven other Nava tapestries behind the altar were based on the description of the New Jerusalem in the book of Revelation. Another Nava tapestry in the baptistery represents the baptism of Jesus by John the Baptist.

On the lower floor is found the Chapel of St. Vibiana. An ancient Roman martyr, she is the patron saint of the archdiocese of Los Angeles, and her relics repose in her shrine in the new cathedral. Adjacent to the chapel is the mausoleum, whose corridors are illuminated by stained glass windows removed from the former cathedral.

Although designed by Spanish architect Jose Rafael Moneo of Madrid, the Cathedral of Our Lady of the Angels is full of references to the past, present, and future of Los Angeles. Moneo constructed the building of architectural concrete in a color which deliberately recalls the original adobe missions of California. It overlooks the Hollywood Freeway, whose unending streams of traffic, Moneo has said, form a "river of transportation," and the 151 million-pound structure is built to withstand an eight-point earthquake.

Although the need for a Roman Catholic cathedral larger than St. Vibiana's,

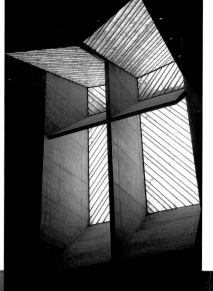

The alabaster altar window features a 60-foot cross

(Above and right) Contemporary vessels for partaking of the Eucharist

The bronze crucifix on the movable cross was sculpted by Simon Toparovsky. The five-ton altar is of Turkish marble supported by a base decorated with four bronze angels by M. L. Snowden.

The formal seat for the archbishop is known as the cathedra. Designed by Jefferson Tortorelli, the cathedra utilizes wood from ten different countries, symbolizing the diverse ethnic communities of Los Angeles.

Twenty-five tapestries by John Nava illustrate the Communion of Saints

OPPOSITE PAGE: The Dobson pipe organ is five stories high, with 6019 pipes.

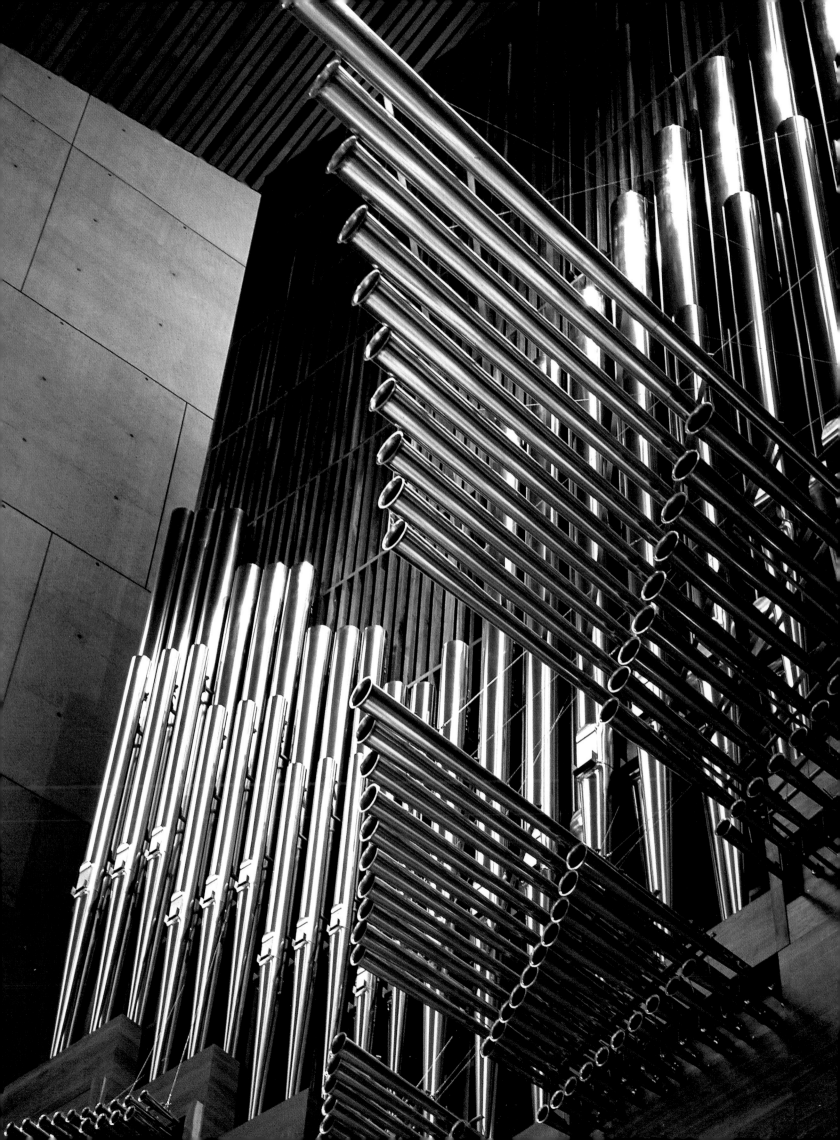

This larger-than-life Madonna is found in one of the side chapels

OPPOSITE PAGE: After extensive restoration, a 300-year-old retablo from Ezcaray, Spain, has a new home in the cathedral

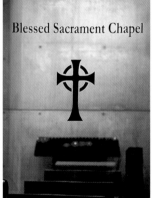

Blessed Sacrament Chapel includes a tabernacle designed by Max DeMoss (below)

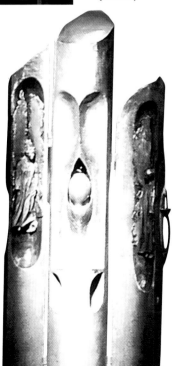

The twelve dedication candle holders represent the twelve tribes of Israel, and were created by Max DeMoss.

Tapestries by John Nava behind the granite baptismal pool designed by Richard Vosko (below) show Jesus' baptism in the River Jordan by John the Baptist (left)

Relics of St. Vibiana, patron saint of the Archdiocese of Los Angeles, rest in a shrine on the lower floor of the cathedral

The baptismal font from the original St. Vibiana Cathedral

The shrine's lighting fixture (above) and lectern (right) are from the earlier cathedral

The chapel of St. Vibiana includes the refurbished altar from the original cathedral showing Jesus as the Lamb of God

The Stations of the Cross which line the walls of the chapel are from St. Vibiana's

The halls of the cathedral's mausoleum are lined with the stained glass windows from the Cathedral of St. Vibiana. Created by the Franz Mayer Studios in Germany in the 1920s, they have been restored by Judson Studios.

OPPOSITE PAGE: Etched with a band of sixteen angels, the Donor Wall includes the names of major benefactors to Our Lady of the Angels. It was created by Judson Studios.

CHRIST THE KING
ROMAN CATHOLIC CHURCH

Christ the King Roman Catholic Church,
Los Angeles

RIGHT: Paintings on tile
decorate the exterior
courtyard of the church

OPPOSITE PAGE: The figure
of Christ in the reredos
is crowned

The baptismal
font in the
narthex of
the church

In 1922, Pope Pius XI issued an encyclical decree stating that the most effective way to establish peace on earth was to restore the reign of Christ the King of all nations. In 1925 the first feast of Christ the King was celebrated, and the next year, when Los Angeles archbishop John J. Cantwell selected a name for a new parish between Western and Highland avenues and Beverly and Santa Monica boulevards, he chose "Christ the King."

The new parish church was built near the intersection of Melrose and Rossmore avenues. Services were first held in a house on Arden Boulevard, while architect Thomas Franklin Power drew plans for the new church, to be modeled after the Basilica of St. Sophia in Constantinople and St. Mark's Cathedral in Venice. By 1927 the new church was dedicated, although it was not until 1947 that the decoration was completed.

The stained glass windows were designed by Joseph Tierney. Christ the King is the theme of the trio of windows in the apse above the altar. Along the aisles, four windows of the four evangelists are surrounded by stained glass designs and symbols from the life of Christ. These symbols were created by Tierney, and include such devices as three crowns for the Magi, symbol of the Epiphany; a lotus flower and pyramid as reminders of the Holy Family's flight into Egypt; a branched candlestick recalling Jesus as a young boy conversing with the elders of the temple; carpenter's tools indicating his early occupation, and a basket of bread loaves as a symbol of feeding the multitudes.

Belgian artist L.G. Marissael, who trained at the Catholic Art School in Ghent, was commissioned to paint six murals in arched alcoves beneath the church windows. His theme is episodes from the life of Christ.

Set into niches on both sides of the church are statues of St. Therese, St. Anne, St. Anthony and St. Patrick. To celebrate the church's silver anniversary in 1951, parishioners donated a twelve-foot Italian marble statue of Christ the King, sculpted by A.J. Arany, to be placed outside the church, facing the Hollywood Hills. In one hand Christ holds the scepter of authority; in the other a globe, symbolizing a universe redeemed.

OPPOSITE PAGE: **Christ the King is the theme of the three windows in the apse**

Mosaic images in the Mary Altar

St. Gennero, patron saint of Naples

LEFT AND ABOVE: **Antique implements for sacramental observances**

The Stations of the Cross are in niches along the walls

A Tree of Virtues in a wall niche

Painted murals below the stained glass windows illustrate scenes from the life of Christ

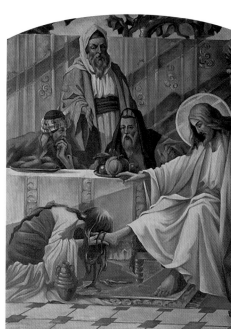

Detail of a tabernacle door in the Mary Altar

Madonna and Child

The Lamb of God painted in the center of the Sanctuary arch

CHURCH OF ST. CHARLES BORROMEO

Church of St. Charles Borromeo,
North Hollywood

TOP RIGHT: A light in
the baptistery

OPPOSITE PAGE: The Dream of
St. Joseph window on the
west wall of the church

Much of the stained
glass was executed by the
Paul L. Phillips Studio

The patron saint of the Church of St. Charles Borromeo was a 16th century cardinal of Milan, Italy, who was noted not only for his diplomatic and administrative skills, but for his compassion when the people of Milan were beset first by famine and then by plague.

The North Hollywood parish began with services held in private homes in the late 1800s, when the area was known as Lankershim. In the early 1920s, the congregation bought a Methodist church at the corner of Weddington and Bakman streets which was renamed Immaculate Conception Church. In 1925 the name was changed to the Church of St. Charles Borromeo. Although the church later expanded onto adjacent property, ground for a new building was purchased on Moorpark Street and the new church, designed by Laurence Viole, was completed in 1938 at a cost of $50,000. In 1952, at a cost of $110,000, the land for the present church was purchased.

Designed by J. Earl Trudeau in the Spanish Colonial style, the church

opened on Thanksgiving Day, 1959. The façade of the building is highlighted by the Borromean Window, illustrating scenes from the life of the church's patron saint in stained glass. Above the window is his motto, "Humilitas." The Spanish crucifix over the altar, the altar table and lectern of hand-carved wood were all

previously in the former church. The painted Stations of the Cross were executed by St. Charles parishioner Judith Serbaroli.

The Jesse Tree stained glass window on the east side of the church represents David, Solomon, and other ancestors of Jesus as described in the book of Isaiah. On the highest branch are the Madonna and Child, and the Jesse Tree is flanked by figures of prophets. The Dream of St. Joseph is the subject of the opposite window, on the west side of the church. St. Joseph is at the bottom of the window, with events in the life of Jesus above him. On either side are the evangelists and the epistolarians.

The late comedian Bob Hope and his wife Dolores donated Our Lady's Chapel to the church at the time of its construction. Redecorated in the 1980s, it now features an altar of Italian marble inset with faux lapis lazuli.

Our Lady's Chapel was a gift from Dolores and Bob Hope

OPPOSITE PAGE: The altar table and lectern were fashioned of wood from the congregation's previous church

The chapel's tabernacle

A shrine to St. Joseph

The Stations of the Cross were painted by Judith Serbaroli

CHURCH OF THE ANGELS

Church of the Angels, Pasadena

RIGHT: **The Campbell-Johnston family donated the angel sundial**

OPPOSITE PAGE: **A detail of the pulpit**

Leaded windows beside the pulpit

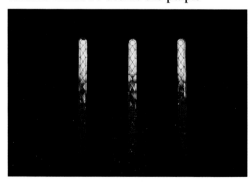

Alexander Campbell-Johnston was a Scotsman who purchased and developed most of Rancho San Rafael in the 19th century. As a memorial to her late husband, his wife decided to build a church to serve the Episcopalian worshipers of the village of Garvanza in what is now Pasadena.

Mrs. Campbell-Johnston traveled to England to choose the architect for what would become Church of the Angels. She selected Arthur Edmund Street, the son of Victorian architect George E. Street, who was noted for his design of Holmbury St. Mary's Church in Dorking, England. This building served as the basis for Arthur Street's design for Church of the Angels.

Back in America, Street's plans were revised by Ernest A. Coxhead, who designed much of the Episcopalian Church architecture in California. The cornerstone for Church of the Angels was laid on Easter Eve, 1889, and the church was consecrated five months later. Since 1889 the Bishop of Los Angeles has been the church's rector, with his chaplain serving as vicar.

The building's façade includes red sandstone from Rancho San Rafael, and is faced with sandstone from the San Fernando Valley. An eight-day Seth Thomas clock strikes the hour in the 44-foot belfry. In memory of their mother, the sons of Mrs. Campbell-Johnston donated a stone sundial set within heart-shaped landscaping.

The workmen who built Church of the Angels donated the baptistery font of Mexican alabaster and Italian marble. The memorial window illustrating Jesus' open tomb on Easter morning was designed in London, as was the lectern representing Archangel St. Michael. This was designed by English sculptor W.R. Ingram, and carved in Belgium from single piece of 400-year-old oak. The olive wood veneer of the altar and furniture of the chancel is from the grounds of Mission San Gabriel. The pipe organ is original to the church, built and installed in 1889, while the pulpit, carved of English oak with a base of Portland stone, celebrates the 40th anniversary of Church of the Angels.

The interior of the church is red pressed brick

RIGHT: A lectern of Archangel Michael was designed by sculptor W.R. Ingram

FAR RIGHT: The ceiling is redwood

CHURCH OF THE ANGELS

A view of the altar from the baptistery

The baptismal
font was donated
by the workmen
who built the
church

The English oak pulpit
was installed at the
40th anniversary of
Church of the Angels

Columns in the Sanctuary

A rain gutter bears a cross

Detail of a door hinge

The Campbell-Johnston crypt on the church grounds

OPPOSITE PAGE: The memorial window represents the discovery of Jesus' open tomb on Easter

The crypt cornerstone

CHURCH OF THE BLESSED SACRAMENT

Church of the Blessed Sacrament, Hollywood

RIGHT: **A marble sculpture shows Jesus giving Holy Communion to St. John**

OPPOSITE PAGE: **The shrine to St. Anthony**

The 1920s were a time of major church building throughout Los Angeles, when many of the city's religious denominations planned massive edifices in a variety of architectural styles. But with the advent of the Depression followed by World War II, congregations which had begun ambitious building projects were often forced to wait years before their structures were completed and/or paid for.

The Church of the Blessed Sacrament was one of these. Begun in 1927, the Spanish Colonial Renaissance-style church, with a seating capacity of 1500, was designed by the Beezer Brothers firm of San Francisco. By the time of its dedication in 1928, the building had a roof and enclosed walls, so services commenced in the unfinished church. With the shortage of funds and materials during the Depression and war, construction ground to a halt in 1929 and was not resumed until 1952.

Built of reinforced concrete, Blessed Sacrament's tower and roof supports are of steel. Two exterior niches contain statues of St. Thomas Aquinas and St. Clare of Assisi.

A decorative theme within the interior is undulating parallel lines and groups of radiating leaves. These symbolize water and life, specifically the waters of grace and the life of the soul which grace produces. The marble of the Sanctuary columns is alternately brown Colorado colorosa and cream Italian travertine. Also of Italian marble is the baptistery font, which was contributed by the children of the Blessed Sacrament school.

The Stations of the Cross, painted in semi-circular panels, were created by Italian artist Carlo Wostry, who began them in Italy and later finished the series in the Heinsbergen Studios in Hollywood in the 1930s. The largest of the side altar chapels is Our Lady's Chapel, with its own set of pews for special devotions. The background to the statue of the Virgin Mary is Venetian mosaic. Above the crest of the central altar niche is a marble cross with a bronze statue of Christ. A gold-leaf sunburst forms the altar canopy.

Two balconies overlook the Sanctuary. One is soundproofed for mothers and small children; the other houses the organ, which was donated by singer Bing Crosby, and accommodations for the choir.

Archangel Michael with his double-edged sword of truth

The choir loft houses the organ and console

The ceiling of the apse

OPPOSITE PAGE: The church is 280 feet long and 104 feet wide

Detail of the pulpit

The 1200-pound marble baptismal font was a gift from school children to the church

Angels of white Carrara marble embellish the main altar

CHURCH OF THE GOOD SHEPHERD

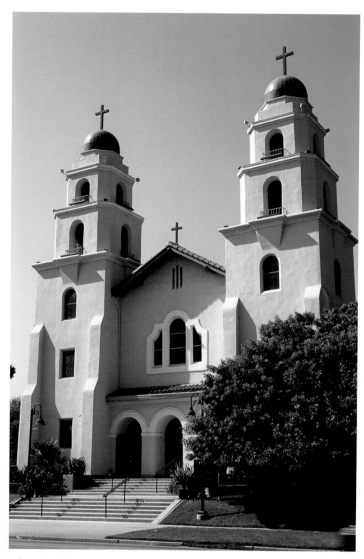

Church of the Good Shepherd, Beverly Hills

RIGHT: **Statues of the Holy Family welcome visitors**

OPPOSITE PAGE: **Relics of saints are sealed in the altar**

The Roman Catholic parish of the Church of the Good Shepherd began in 1923, in what was then the nine-year-old suburban community of Beverly Hills. Noting the area's concentration of movie stars and other film industry notables, Bishop John J. Cantwell instructed the Good Shepherd pastor, Michael Mullins, to form the Catholic Motion Picture Guild. Soon both church and guild were supported by the likes of Jackie Coogan and Ben Turpin, and later such stars as Ray Bolger, Jimmy Durante, Loretta Young, Rosalind Russell and Gene Kelly. Although worshippers in the new parish first met for Mass in an apartment building and later the Beverly Hills Hotel, throughout 1924 the Mission-style church and rectory were under construction on N. Bedford Drive. Designed by J.J. Donellan, the frame and stucco building was dedicated in 1925 and substantially renovated in 1959, when a new marble main altar and two side altars were added. Sealed in each altar are relics of St. Felicitas, St. Perpetua, and St. Vibiana, the patroness of the

Los Angeles diocese.

During the 1959 renovation, the Paul Phillips Studio replaced many of the original landscapes in the stained glass windows which line the church. Subjects of the windows include St. John the Evangelist, St. Patrick, St. Joseph, St. Paul, Jesus as the Good Shepherd, the Virgin Mary, the Sacred Heart of Jesus, St. Peter, St. Michael the Archangel, St. Anthony of Padua, and St. Anne.

The church was substantially
renovated in 1959

The tabernacle

RIGHT: The carved
altar crucifix

FAR RIGHT: Madonna and Child

TOP RIGHT: **Jesus** blesses the congregation

Stained glass cherubs

Doric columns form the ambulatory

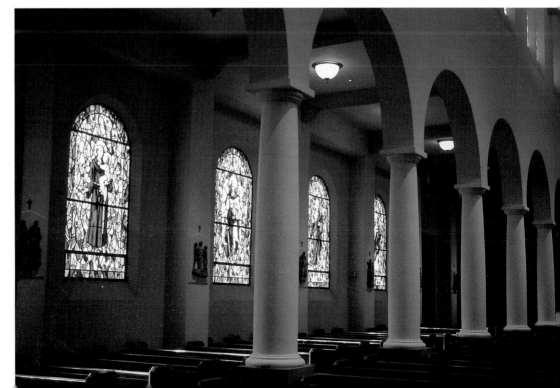

CHURCH OF THE GOOD SHEPHERD

Many of the stained glass windows
were redesigned by the Paul Phillips
Studio in the 1959 renovation

The Stations of the Cross line the aisles

A carving of the Sacred Heart of Jesus

OPPOSITE PAGE: St. Joseph and Jesus at the baptismal font

The altar to the Virgin Mary

FIRST AFRICAN METHODIST EPISCOPAL CHURCH OF LOS ANGELES

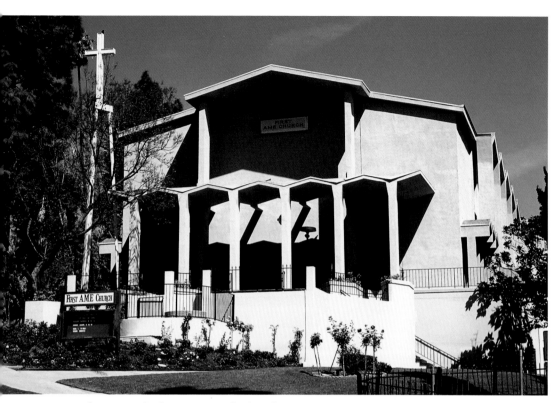

First African Methodist Episcopal Church of Los Angeles

OPPOSITE PAGE: "God and Us," a massive mural by Eddie L. Edwards, dominates the church interior

OVERLEAF: The "God and Us" mural includes (from upper left) the culture and contributions of Africans, and (upper right) American individuals such as Richard Allen who forwarded the cause of individual and religious freedom in America.

Church pioneer Biddy Mason

First A.M.E. Church of Los Angeles sprang to national attention during the Los Angeles civil unrest of 1992. Members of the church provided physical protection for the city's police and fire fighters, as well as shelter, food and myriad services for the community during this troubled time. These activities, and the leadership of senior minister Cecil Murray, made First A.M.E. a media focus.

The church is located in Sugar Hill, an affluent black neighborhood which, over the years, was the home of such stars as Lena Horne, Dorothy Dandridge, Hattie McDaniel, and Johnny Mathis. Many of its beautiful houses have been purchased by First A.M.E. as part of its ongoing expansion and community economic development campaign. Throughout the years, the church had been quietly forwarding independent business growth, housing, and educational programs in the community.

The current church, whose cornerstone is dated 1968, is only the third home for the congregation since it was founded in the home of Bridget "Biddy" Mason, 1818-1891. She was a former slave who had followed her Mormon owners on foot, herding their cattle, when they moved from Mississippi to Utah and finally to San Bernardino. Mason successfully petitioned for her freedom in California, which was a free state. She practiced nursing and midwifery and eventually owned valuable real estate in downtown Los Angeles.

She was inspired to found the first A.M.E. church in the west by the historic example of Richard Allen, 1760-1831, a slave who converted to Methodism and eventually purchased his own freedom from his Philadelphia owners. When he and his followers were refused the right to worship in a church they had helped to build, Allen began the A.M.E. church in a blacksmith's shop, where his first pulpit was an anvil. Today the A.M.E. denomination has a national membership of more than a million followers.

A massive mural by painter Eddie L. Edwards is the centerpiece of the Sanctuary at First A.M.E. Church of Los Angeles, honoring Allen, Mason, and other individuals and symbols of the history of the A.M.E. church. Prominent figures represented in the mural include abolitionist Frederick Douglass and Rev. Hiram Revels, the first black United States senator. At the center of the painting is a reference to the Christian Recorder newspaper, the oldest black religious weekly in the country, which the A.M.E. church began publishing in 1841. Stained glass windows depict contemporary African-American leaders such as Martin Luther King Jr. and Rosa Parks as well as Richard Allen and numerous saints.

The church's stained glass windows celebrate contemporary figures such as Martin Luther King Jr. and Robert and John F. Kennedy as well as Old and New Testament figures (opposite page).

FIRST BAPTIST CHURCH
OF LOS ANGELES

First Baptist Church of Los Angeles

**Windows in the
Moore Prayer Chapel**

Some of the most prominent names in the history of Southern California are linked to the history of First Baptist Church of Los Angeles. Isaac Lankershim, who owned most of the southern half of the San Fernando Valley, was an organizer of the original congregation in 1874, and served as one of its trustees; the Lankershim family continued its sponsorship of the church for many years. Developer and hotel owner Isaac Newton Van Nuys, who managed Lankershim's property and married his daughter, was also a First Baptist trustee. Among other contributions, the Van Nuys family paid for a cement sidewalk in front of First Baptist's original building on Sixth Street. Susan Miller Dorsey, the wife of one of the early pastors of the church, served as superintendent of Los Angeles Schools; the city's Dorsey High is named after her.

As well as its extensive foreign missionary outreach, the church has always been deeply involved in philanthropic and social services to the city. First Baptist sponsored a Chinese mission to provide support for the thousands of Chinese who came to Southern California to build the railways and stayed to work in the laundries, as domestics, and vegetable and fish distributors. It also ran the Berean Mission, which provided vocational training for young people.

First Baptist's original home at Sixth and Fort (now Broadway) streets was dedicated in 1884. The current church was designed by the firm of Allison and Allison and completed in 1927 at a cost of $650,000. The 130-room edifice is considered surprisingly ornate for a Baptist church. The gold-leaf, coffered ceiling of the Sanctuary is an adaptation of that in the chapel of the ducal palace in Montava, Italy. The church's three rose windows were inspired by those of Chartres Cathedral. The nave windows represent the life of Christ, the twelve apostles, and the law and Old Testament prophets.

The plaster walls and "theatre"-style seating, instead of pews, were the choice of the congregation. The 155-foot bell tower is known as Crowell Tower, named after Weymouth Crowell, builder of the church.

The ceiling of the Sanctuary is a copy of that in the ducal chapel in Montava, Italy

LEFT: One of three rose windows which are copies of those in Chartres Cathedral in France

A detail of the coffered ceiling, finished in gold leaf

A transept window

72

Stained glass windows (left and above) were added to Francis Chapel in the 1950s

The carving of Christ in Francis Chapel is by Miriam Shelton Dean

FIRST CONGREGATIONAL CHURCH OF LOS ANGELES

First Congregational Church of Los Angeles

RIGHT: **A symbol of the Christian church**

OPPOSITE PAGE: **The reredos incorporates church symbols, shields and figural carvings, as well as vines, grapes and roses representing Christ and the Resurrection**

The bronze doors were created by Canadian craftsman Albert Gilles

First Congregational Church is known as one of the oldest continuously active Protestant churches in Los Angeles. The first local Congregationalist sermon was preached in a private home in the city in July 1866 and a year later the Congregationalist Society of Los Angeles was formally organized. New High Street was the site of the first meeting house for the followers of the Pilgrim faith. The one-story structure could seat 200 church attendees and was dedicated in 1868.

Subsequent locations for First Congregational were its second church at Third and Hill streets, its third at Sixth and Hill, its fourth at Ninth and Hope. In 1932 the congregation moved to its current home, a cathedral at Sixth Street and Commonwealth Avenue.

Its architects were Allison and Allison, who also designed First Baptist Church of Los Angeles. The medieval Gothic cathedrals, such as Notre Dame, were braced by flying buttresses, but as an example of English Gothic Revival architecture, First Congregational's reinforced concrete structure is supported by 500 tons of steel bars. The church tower rises to a height of 157 feet and is a copy of the tower of Magdalen College, Oxford.

The bronze doors leading to the Sanctuary were added to the building in 1946 to honor Minister James Fifield. Canadian artist Albert Gilles created the doors, which weigh 1,000 pounds each and illustrate scenes from the life of Jesus. Within the Sanctuary, notable for its groin vaulting and carved oak pews, the reredos is inspired by that at Winchester Cathedral. Alois Lang of Obergammergau executed its niche carvings of the four evangelists, the prophet Isaiah, and St. Paul. Carved shields representing various symbols of Christianity and church history are also part of the reredos ornamentation.

Among the themes of the stained glass windows, designed by Judson Studios of Los Angeles, are the clerestory series of Old Testament scenes and the influence of the Holy Spirit. The rose window in the west end of the nave illustrates Christ surrounded by martyrs, prophets, kings and angels. The north balcony window includes scenes from the Old Testament; opposite, in the south transept, is the Apostolic Window. The theme of the smaller windows along both aisles is the miracles of Christ.

TOP, ABOVE AND RIGHT: First Congregational boasts one of the largest church pipe organs in the world, including more than 20,000 pipes

OPPOSITE PAGE: Inspired by European cathedrals, the Sanctuary is 198 feet long

Shadows repeat the delicate Gothic tracery of the stonework

The guilded cross on the main altar of the Sanctuary

OPPOSITE PAGE: The window in Shatto Chapel was designed by Lamb Studios in New York

The Gothic arch recurs throughout First Congregational

FIRST PRESBYTERIAN CHURCH OF HOLLYWOOD

First Presbyterian Church of Hollywood

RIGHT: One of a pair of chancel urns

OPPOSITE PAGE: The organ paneling is carved with the grape and vine motif

The church pulpit

An acre of land in Hollywood sold for $3.00 in 1908, the year the membership of First Presbyterian Church of Hollywood began construction on its first church on Gower Street. Organized in December, 1903, the church had met for five years at the Masonic Temple on Highland Avenue before voting to purchase land and build. But funds were exhausted before the church was completed, so the members held services, Sunday School and social events in their new, flat-roofed basement. The next year the building was completed at a total cost of $15,000, with most of the actual labor done by the church elders and members.

This original building is adjacent to the present church, whose cornerstone was laid in 1923. Architect H.M. Patterson chose the English Gothic style for the foyer and Sanctuary, whose walls and ceilings are covered in zenitherm, a synthetic stone. Openwork oak beams and trusses and hand-painting stenciling lighten the Sanctuary ceiling. The series of stained glass lancet windows in the narthex honors leaders of the Protestant Reformation: John Wycliffe, who translated the Bible into English; John Huss before the Council of Constance, where he was requested to retract his teachings and writings; Martin Luther nailing his theses to the door of Wittenburg Cathedral; John Calvin preaching in Geneva; John Knox denouncing Mary, Queen of Scots; and Huguenot leader Gaspard de Coligni. A shield inset in each window indicates the nationality of each leader.

Stained glass windows also line the Sanctuary, which seats 1800. The theme of the windows under the balcony is Jesus' parables, including "The Lost Sheep," "The Lost Coin," "The Prodigal Son" and "The Sower." The symbols in the windows above the balcony indicate Jesus' names, titles, and offices. The

window in the front of the church above the balcony depicts major events in the lives of leaders of the Presbyterian Church in Europe and the United States. All of the stained glass in the church was executed by Judson Studios.

The oak pulpit is carved with grapes and vines, traditional symbols of Christ and his disciples.

Wylie Chapel was built in 1951, and continues the Gothic style of the church

OPPOSITE PAGE: The Sanctuary seats approximately 1800

The emblems in the balcony window of the main Sanctuary commemorate events in the lives of leaders of the Presbyterian Church throughout Europe and North America

The chapel's Prince of Peace window

The chapel is "Dedicated to the service of the Prince of Peace"

FIRST UNITED METHODIST CHURCH OF NORTH HOLLYWOOD

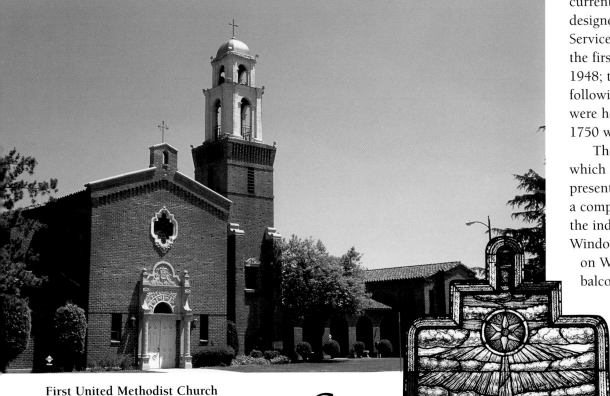

First United Methodist Church
of North Hollywood

RIGHT: **The balcony
windows are from
the congregration's
first church**

OPPOSITE PAGE: **Christ
crowned with thornes**

**The entrance to
the Sanctuary**

Services
for the
Community Church,
which would later
come to be known as First
United Methodist, were first
held in a bunkhouse on
Lankershim Boulevard in
1892. Worship later moved to
the Lankershim (later North
Hollywood) schoolhouse, and
in 1895 the first church was
built at the corner of Bakman
and Weddington streets at a
cost of $735. In 1919 a larger
church was begun on
Lankershim Boulevard and McCormick
Street and completed in 1923.

By 1944 the congregation sold this
building and purchased the present
Tujunga Avenue property of three and a
half acres. After World War II,
volunteers from the church
membership began construction on the

current complex of church buildings,
designed by architect Claude Faithful.
Services were held in the Social Hall,
the first building to be completed, in
1948; the Sanctuary was built the
following year and the first services
were held on Easter Sunday 1949, with
1750 worshippers in attendance.

The pairs of stained glass windows
which line both sides of the church
present the figures of the apostles with
a complementary window illustrating
the individual symbol of each one.
Windows moved from the first church
on Weddington Street adorn the
balcony, and show the child Jesus and
Jesus as the Good Shepherd.

An elaborate wooden
carving of The Last Supper is
the showpiece of the church
altar. Pagodas, exotic flowers,
and Chinese figures depicting
scenes from the life
of Christ surround
the familiar Da
Vinci figures: the
carving was a gift
to the church from
a couple who had
lived near Shanghai
in the 1930s. They
had operated a
funeral parlor next
to an orphanage
where Chinese
boys were taught
the trades of wood
carving, masonry
and metal work
and had watched the students work on
the carving for over a year. When
finished, the school presented it to the
couple, who brought it back to America
a few months before World War II
began, and eventually gave it to First
United Methodist.

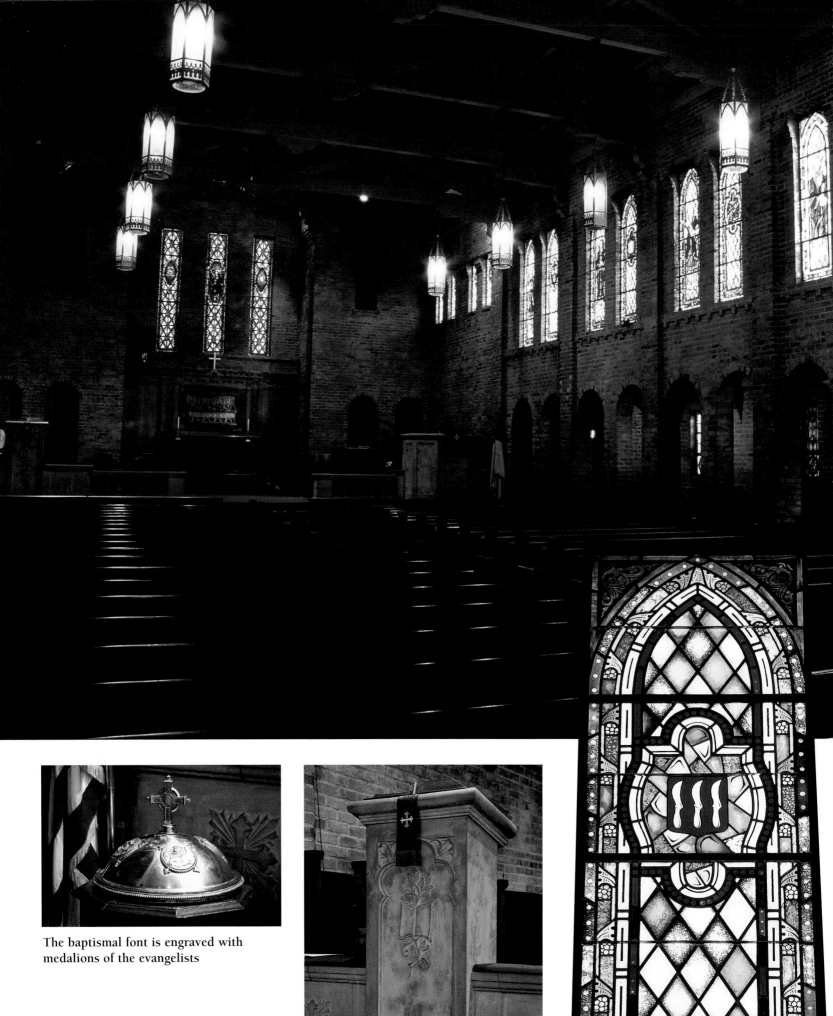

The baptismal font is engraved with medalions of the evangelists

The pulpit

TOP AND LEFT: The carving
of the Last Supper on
the altar was created at a
school in China

The Gothic arch is repeated in windows and lanterns

Built largely by
volunteer labor,
First United
Methodist
seats 500

OPPOSITE PAGE:
Each pair of
windows celebrate
an apostle and his
symbol

A panel dedicated
to the prophet
Hosea

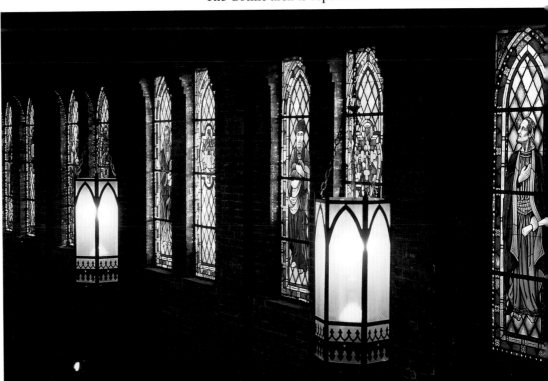

First United Methodist Church of Pasadena

First United Methodist Church
of Pasadena

RIGHT: The cornerstone from the church's
second edifice, dedicated in 1901

OPPOSITE PAGE: Curved pews and
balcony are typical Methodist
church interior features

The church bell
tolled for a
temperance
victory

passed in the city, which was strongly supported by the Methodist congregation. When this ordinance was upheld by the Supreme Court, the church's bell tolled in victorious celebration, but for more than 20 years thereafter, extra ushers were needed to protect the Methodist services and church building from the disruption of anti-temperance demonstrators.

After World War I, the membership of First United Methodist purchased land for a new church edifice on Colorado Boulevard and Oakland Avenue. The English Gothic Revival-style building of 104 rooms was completed in 1924. Its architect was Thomas P. Barber, who would later design First United Methodist Church of Hollywood.

The fan vaulting and decorative plasterwork in the Sanctuary ceiling, which camouflage the ventilation system, frame the pulpit and the E.M. Skinner pipe organ. The stained glass windows on the north, east and west sides of the church were created by the Roy C. Baillie Studios in Los Angeles. They tell the life of Jesus from the Annunciation to the Ascension, and include childhood scenes, illustrated parables, and individual teachings.

In a one-room building on Orange Grove Avenue, lit by kerosene lamps, the first Methodist church in Pasadena was dedicated in 1877. The church could accommodate 200 worshipers, more than eight times the size of the founding congregation. Services were held every other Sunday, as the pastor shared a circuit ministry with San Gabriel and Alhambra.

As Pasadena grew, so did the church's membership, requiring several moves to increasingly larger facilities. By 1886, a temperance ordinance was

The Whittier Narrows earthquake of 1987 caused considerable damage to First United Methodist. The congregation voted to retain the structure and began a campaign to raise the funds to seismically upgrade the building. The Sanctuary was reopened and rededicated in 1992, with other rooms and buildings being completed as funding became available.

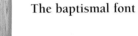

The baptismal font

Stained glass, including a rose window, illumines the chapel

OPPOSITE PAGE AND LEFT: The windows in the Sanctuary depict the life and teachings of Jesus

Elaborate carvings embellish the E. M. Skinner pipe organ.

GOOD SAMARITAN HOSPITAL
ALL SOULS CHAPEL

All Souls Chapel, Los Angeles

OPPOSITE PAGE:
The crucifix over the altar

Votive lights
under a carved
wooden crucifix

The marble
columns are
multicolored

The Hospital of the Good Samaritan began in a cottage in 1885, when a missionary known as Sister Mary Wood was sent to Los Angeles by William Kip, Episcopal Bishop of California. By 1887, Sister Mary's "Los Angeles Hospital and Home for Invalids" was sponsored and expanded by the parish of St. Paul, and given the name "St. Paul's Hospital and Home for Invalids." By the end of the 19th century, the institution had become "The Hospital of the Good Samaritan" overseen not by a single parish, but by the Episcopal Diocese of Los Angeles.

In 1927, after Good Samaritan had consolidated resources with Columbia Hospital Association, a new hospital wing was added which included a chapel building.

The architect for the new building, including the chapel, was Reginald Johnson, son of Joseph Johnson, first bishop of the Episcopal Diocese of Los Angeles. He conceived the hospital chapel as a miniature version of St. Paul's Cathedral at Wilshire Boulevard and Figueroa Street, which he also designed. (The cathedral was demolished for seismic considerations in 1980).

Twelve multi-colored marble columns form ambulatories the length of the chapel. The tile floors are convenient for patients in wheelchairs who attend services, and in a 1927 hospital annual report, it was noted that "Not infrequently, patients are brought in their beds, an advantage probably not offered at any other church service in Los Angeles…The most interesting service of the week is that on Friday evening, when all nurses not on duty are expected to be present, and the chapel is well filled with nurses in uniform."

GOOD SHEPHERD CENTER FOR HOMELESS WOMEN
IRENE WIERMAN CHAPEL

The chapel is inside the Administrative
Center of the Women's Village

St. Joseph is the patron saint of the Sisters
who administer Good Shepherd

The Women's Village is raising Los Angeles' awareness of the need – and the possibilities – of helping hundreds of the city's homeless women and their children.

In 1984, under the auspices of Los Angeles Catholic Charities, the Good Shepherd Center for Homeless Women began. The Languille Residence, Good Shepherd's first drop-in center in downtown Los Angeles, supplied a safe haven where needy women could find temporary shelter, hot meals, showers, clothing, and counseling.

A non-denominational, volunteer board of 20 women and men supported Sr. Julia Mary Farley, the program's administrator, as Good Shepherd's services expanded over the years to include transitional housing and a residence for homeless mothers and their children.

But Sr. Julia Mary's vision continued to expand. By 1994, her goal was a Women's Village providing transitional housing for homeless women, affordable housing for the handicapped homeless, permanent housing, and retail facilities to train women for employment. By 1996, Good Shepherd had purchased a complex of homes on Rockwood Street and ground was broken for the Women's Village.

Integral to the plan for the Village was a chapel, to provide a quiet place for prayer and meditation. It is located in a 1915 brick building, original to the property, which also houses the Village's Administrative Center. Before any demolition or construction on any of the other buildings began, donations of furnishings began to pour in for the chapel; it was completely furnished before a single brick was moved to begin building the Women's Village.

When St. Timothy's convent was being closed, Bishop Ward offered the furniture to Good Shepherd Center for Homeless Women. He also contributed an altar, whose recessed altar stone contains the relics of Egyptian martyrs. Paul Wierman donated the chairs. Kathy Baumgardner donated the organ and Betsy and Thomas Coleman presented the Village with four 16th century stained glass windows, which were restored by artisans from the Jerry Shorrock Studios who cleaned more than 2500 individual pieces of stained glass and replaced all the leading in each window.

Four 16th century stained glass windows are the showpiece of the chapel

The chapel was furnished entirely by donations

Statues of the Virgin Mary and
St. Joseph flank the altar

HOLY FAMILY CATHOLIC CHURCH

Holy Family Catholic Church,
South Pasadena

RIGHT: **Jesus portrayed
in stained glass**

OPPOSITE PAGE:
**St. Columbkill in a niche
in the reredos**

The rose window

A cottage on El Centro Avenue was the site of the first Holy Family Church in the city of South Pasadena; Mass was first celebrated there in 1910. The cottage was soon replaced by a bungalow church and in 1923 the parish moved this structure to a lot at Fremont Drive and Rollin Street. Holy Family had earlier purchased this land as the site of a new church to accommodate the growing congregation.

After years of bazaars, picnics, car washes, bake sales, card parties and dances, the church had raised sufficient funds to hire an architect to design its new home. Emmet G. Martin was chosen as architect. He began construction in 1927, the same year he completed building St. Brendan Catholic Church in Los Angeles.

For Holy Family, Martin designed a church in the Spanish Baroque style, with a 90-foot bell tower surmounted by a Moorish tiled dome. Carved stone ornamentation is a characteristic of the Spanish Baroque, and is found at the church's entry portals and above the north and south transept windows. The building's façade includes bronze figures of the Holy Family and two bas-relief stone medallions depicting the boyhood of Jesus. Each of the mahogany pews is carved with a cross, heart and crown.

In 1950, the mahogany side altars were installed, and the next year Hector Serbaroli and his daughter Judith painted murals above each altar. The ceramic magnificat was created by Isabelle Piczek.

In 1962, stained glass windows were imported from France to line both sides of the Sanctuary and celebrate events in the life of Jesus, the apostles, and other saints with special significance to the Holy Family Church.

Schoenstein & Company installed the church's organ in 1992. One independent pedal organ was situated near the front of the Sanctuary, with the main instrument located in the balcony, allowing music to emanate from two positions within the church.

The Sanctuary
seats nearly
700

Detail of the
organ pipes
and rose
window

The carved
wooden pulpit

HOLY FAMILY CATHOLIC CHURCH

The altar cross

The stained glass
windows are French,
and were installed
in 1962

A painting of the
Holy Family in
the reredos

A niche painting in the baptistery

The baptistery

ABOVE RIGHT: The Holy Family in the carpentry shop

The baptismal font

OPPOSITE PAGE: The altar was separated from the reredos in 1970, in accordance with the Vatican II Council

A pieta in the baptistery

HOLY VIRGIN MARY
RUSSIAN ORTHODOX CATHEDRAL

**Holy Virgin Mary Russian
Orthodox Cathedral, Los Angeles**

RIGHT: **Traditional
incense lampadas**

OPPOSITE PAGE: **A crucifix
painted in Byzantine style**

**Listing of the hours
of services**

The cathedral of the Holy Virgin Mary was named after her Russian Orthodox icon, which means "Rescuer of the Perishing Ones." It was an appropriate choice, as the church was founded in 1922 by Russian immigrants fleeing the post-World War I chaos in Europe as well as the Russian Revolution of 1917. At that time, there were only three Orthodox churches on the west coast of America, none of which were in Los Angeles.

The Holy Virgin Mary congregation originally met in a former Episcopal church and hall. A Ladies' Society organized fund raising activities to purchase icons, vestments for the priest, and for the general beautification of the church the parish dreamed of building.

There were few wealthy members of the congregation; most of the parishioners, many of whom had served as officers in the Russian army and navy, spoke little English and worked in factories, as laborers or as domestics.

Nevertheless, in 1928, the membership purchased two lots on Micheltorena Street and church building commenced. The architect, A.A. Tolubeyev, designed the church in the 12-13th century Pskov style of northern Russia. This traditionally included heavy lattice shutters at each window, with most of the interior lighting supplied by candles. As the congregation stands during the service, few seats are provided, to be used by the elderly or infirm. The garden was planted with birch and spruce trees, a reference to the forests of northern Russia.

By 1960 the church was enlarged to almost twice its original size according to a design by B.A. Filippov. A new altar screen and choir stalls (all music in the services is sung or chanted a cappella; no musical instruments are played) were added. In 1971 it was designated a cathedral by the Holy Synod of the Orthodox Church in America. That same year architect S.N. Koschin designed a new building to include the Chapel of St. Herman of Alaska, a school building and sacristy.

An icon of the Mystical Supper

LEFT AND RIGHT: Gilded examples of the
Byzantine cross

LEFT: The icon screen was painted in America by Vladimir Krassovsky

A screen of painted saints surrounded by the Christian symbol of the grapevine

BELOW: Artifacts, icons and ornaments were bequeathed and donated to the church by its members, including the icon of St. George (middle) given by veterans of World War I and the Russian Revolution. St. George was the patron saint of the Imperial Navy.

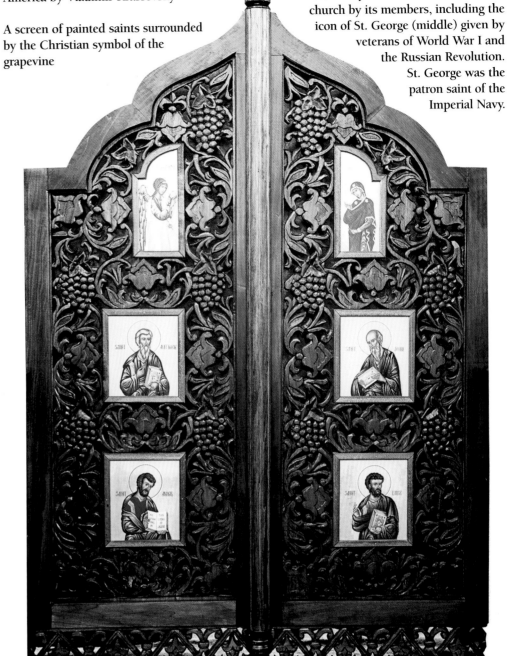

Icons contemporary
and antique fill
the cathedral

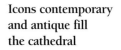

OPPOSITE PAGE: **Our Lady of Tikhvin**
is a copy of an icon painted in 1914
on Mt. Athos as a gift from the Czar

IMMANUEL PRESBYTERIAN CHURCH

Immanuel Presbyterian Church, Los Angeles

Iron crosses are an ancient motif incorporated into the church floors

OPPOSITE PAGE: **The Sanctuary's vaulted ceiling was inspired by English Gothic architecture**

Founded in 1888, the Immanuel Presbyterian congregation built its first church home at the corner of Tenth and Pearl streets in downtown Los Angeles. By 1925 the membership had grown so extensively that blueprints were drawn for a beautiful new church in the same locale that would accommodate the burgeoning membership. But in the midst of these plans came the news that the City of Los Angeles had filed condemnation suits against 3,000 property owners, including the church, whose real estate fronted Tenth Street; the street was going to be enlarged to become a boulevard which would run the length of Los Angeles. Tenth Street would be renamed Olympic Boulevard, Pearl Street became Figueroa Street, and Immanuel Presbyterian, which stood to lose 50 feet of frontage along Figueroa, had to look for a new location.

The New Church Building Committee selected a lot on Wilshire Boulevard and Berendo Street. A member of the congregation, Chauncey F. Skilling, principle in the architectural firm Patterson and Skilling, was chosen as the architect for the 200-room building. The budget for the church, including the Sanctuary, two chapels, meeting and office space on four levels, and the 62-rank E.M. Skinner organ, was $1,400,000. After more than two years of construction, the church was completed in May 1929, just a few months before the Great Depression began; it would be 20 years before the mortgage was paid off.

The French Gothic-style exterior of Immanuel Presbyterian is finished in cast stone. The interior, inspired by 15th century English Gothic architecture, includes the Sanctuary's 80-foot vaulted ceilings and stained glass windows depicting the 12 disciples designed by the Los Angeles Art Glass Company. The historic Malibu Tile Company created the tile floors of the Sanctuary.

Throughout the church, Skilling repeated such symbolic motifs as the quatrefoil, symbol of the four evangelists and four gospels; the trefoil, representing the Holy Trinity; the vine with leaves, branches and clusters of grapes as a reference to Jesus' declaration that he is the true vine; the rose as a symbol of martyrdom, divine law and messianic hope; and the fleur de lys, representing the Holy Trinity.

The marble baptismal font is octagonal, symbolizing regeneration

The historic Malibu Tile Company created the floors of the Sanctuary

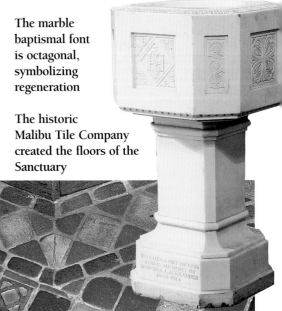

Stone tracery forms a quatrefoil, representing the four evangelists and the four gospels, around the stained glass windows of the Sanctuary

LEFT: The Sanctuary accommodates 2,000 people

Detail of a bas-relief panel

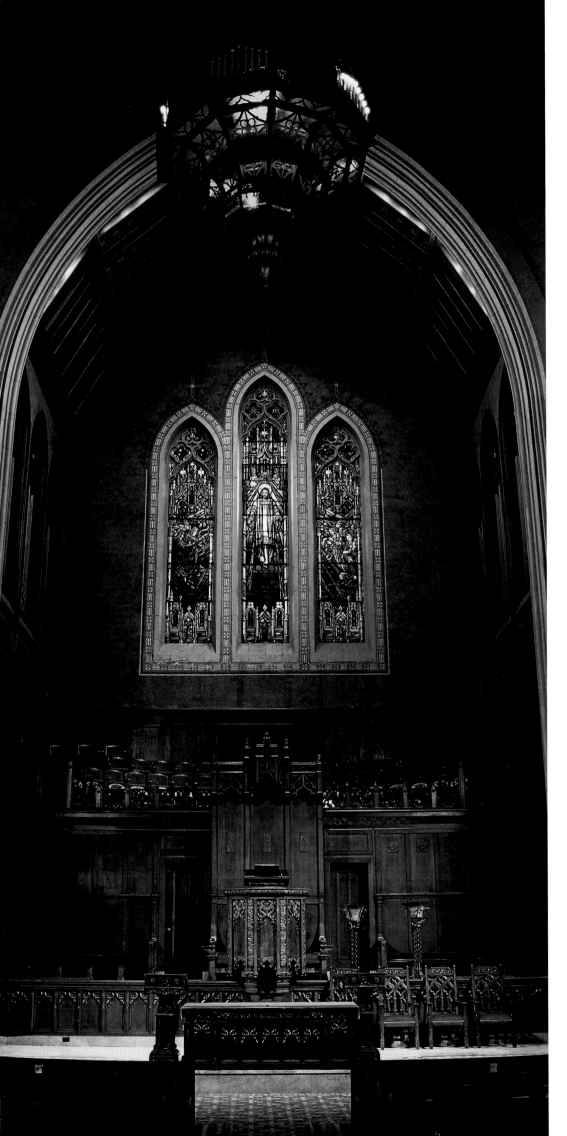

Carvings of roses, symbol of the Virgin Mary, and grape clusters and leaves, symbolizing Christ and his disciples.

LEFT: The Ascension is the subject of the windows above the choir loft

OPPOSITE PAGE: The Rose and Nativity windows are above the main entrance to the Sanctuary

OVERLEAF: The east windows show Jesus blessing little children

IMMANUEL PRESBYTERIAN CHURCH

A smaller rose window is the balcony jewel in Immanuel's Chichester Chapel

The Chichester Chapel organ has a mechanical key and stop action

RIGHT: A detail of the organ decoration

LEFT: Chapel windows illustrating incidents in the life of Christ include the six-pointed ruby star, symbolizing Jesus as the Savior of Mankind

The fleur de lys motif is woven into a fabric hanging beside the organ

LOYOLA MARYMOUNT UNIVERSITY
SACRED HEART CHAPEL

Sacred Heart Chapel, Los Angeles

RIGHT: "Fiat," a bronze by Michael Mullen, is dedicated to the Madonna and to LMU mothers

OPPOSITE PAGE: The altar of red oak and inlaid black walnut was crafted by Donald Engh

In the late 1920s, land developer Harry Culver decided that an academic institution would be an attractive addition to the new city he was building in the barley fields of Westchester. He offered 100 acres of land to the all-male Loyola College if the school would relocate from downtown Los Angeles to the fledgling Culver City. They agreed and ground for the new campus was broken in 1928.

Officially founded in 1911, Loyola's immediate predecessor was St. Vincent's College, which began in 1865. The school is named after St. Ignatius of Loyola, a 16th century Spanish monk who started the Society of Jesus, or Jesuit, order.

The Spanish Colonial Revival-style Sacred Heart Chapel was built in 1953 and designed by M. L. Barker and G.

Lawrence. Its interior celebrates the sainthood and academic accomplishments of the Jesuits in a series of 29 stained glass windows that provides the chapel's primary color and decorative source. When Loyola merged with Marymount University in 1973, additional windows were added in the Francis Xavier chapel to commemorate women saints.

The Sacred Heart Chapel itself was the gift of the three Desmond sisters, whose family owned a department store in Los Angeles' Miracle Mile district. One of the sisters, Anna Desmond, underwrote the cost of the chapel's rose window. In the northern end of the apse, the Christ the King window stands on a base section of stained glass which includes the coat of arms of Loyola Marymount University. On either side of this window are others honoring the Blessed Virgin and St. Joseph, under which are the seals of Santa Clara and the University of San Francisco, both Jesuit colleges in California. Beginning with the west wall of the Sanctuary, additional windows illustrate individual Jesuit saints in order of their canonization. Beneath each is a stained glass panel representing one of the American Jesuit universities and colleges in the order of their founding.

Four other windows include symbols of the original schools of Loyola college: law, engineering, business and liberal arts. The unusual Stations of the Cross are mosaic and depict only the faces of Christ, his tormentors, and the other individuals in the story. In the Mary Chapel, behind Sacred Heart's main altar, is a bronze sculpture of the Heart of Mary by Italian sculptor Francesco Nagni.

The theme of the rose window by Dolci is "The Sacred Heart"

TOP: Stained glass windows celebrate Jesuit saints, colleges, and the Vatican

A lower window commemorates great thinkers throughout history

A mosaic Station of the Cross

The crucifix over the altar

FAR LEFT: The King of Kings window hangs in the apse of the chapel

LEFT: Women saints were honored in the chapel when Loyola merged with Marymount University in 1973

LOYOLA MARYMOUNT UNIVERSITY
HUESMAN CHAPEL

The interior of Huesman Chapel

RIGHT: A ceramic Our Lady of Guadalupe by Mary Ellen McDermott

The stained glass windows were installed in the chapel in 1992.

When the Huesman family donated a dormitory to Loyola Marymount University, a term of the contribution was that the new building contain a chapel. Small and informal, the space is illuminated by a series of four stained glass windows designed by Sr. Genevieve Underwood R.S.H.M., a retired LMU professor of art.

Collectively the theme of the windows is "A Celebration of Praise." A fifth window with a figurative theme is entitled "The Family," and was also designed by Sr. Genevieve. All the windows are made of faceted glass, which is cast rather than blown, set in epoxy resin.

A statue of Our Lady of Guadalupe was created for the chapel.

LOYOLA MARYMOUNT UNIVERSITY
THE JESUIT COMMUNITY CHAPEL

The interior of The Jesuit
Community Chapel

RIGHT: **An Italian carving
of St. Joseph and Jesus**

FAR RIGHT:
**Ignatius
of Loyola**

This small chapel on
the Loyola-Marymount
campus is for the exclusive
use of the Jesuit
community and faculty,
and is not open to the
public. A gift from oil
magnate Edward Doheny,
it is the oldest structure on
the school grounds. After a
previous attempt at updating the chapel,
which involved orange shag carpeting and
raw redwood walls, the interior has been
restored to its original design of stucco
walls, with handmade wrought iron
lighting fixtures and font for holy water.
The atrium which fills the room with light
was the original altar for the chapel.

PEPPERDINE UNIVERSITY
STAUFFER CHAPEL

Stauffer Chapel

An Easter lily in stained glass

Acollege guided by Christian ethics and ideals was the vision of George Pepperdine when he established his college in 1937. The founder of Western Auto Supply Company and a lifelong member of the Churches of Christ, Pepperdine began his undergraduate school in South Central Los Angeles. When its business and education departments became separate schools, and with the addition of a law school, Pepperdine was designated a university. In 1972 it moved to an 830-acre campus in Malibu, and Stauffer Chapel was dedicated the next year.

The chapel was a gift of Beverly Stauffer and designed by architect Ulysses Floyd Rible. More than 3,000 square feet of stained glass in abstract designs, created by Robert Donovan, provide the light and color for the building. The white ash pews seat 180, and an organ is contained within a small balcony. The chapel is a favorite for weddings.

The front window of the chapel faces south,
ensuring light most of the day

The chapel seats 180

Naturalist vignettes among the abstract stained glass designs

ST. ALBAN'S EPISCOPAL CHURCH

St. Alban's Episcopal Church, Westwood

RIGHT: A copy of Michelangelo's "Pieta" in the church courtyard

OPPOSITE PAGE: A lion guards the church's exterior

The support for a downspout is a bird feeding its young

Alban was a Roman soldier stationed in the province of Verulamium (England) in the year 304 A.D. Tradition maintains he sheltered a Christian priest who was fleeing persecution by exchanging clothing with him. Alban was converted to Christianity, baptized and beheaded for his convictions, thus becoming the first man in England to die for Christ.

The St. Alban's Chapel was established at its Westwood location for its proximity to UCLA. Built in 1931 as a memorial to Bishop Joseph Horsfall Johnson, the first Episcopal bishop of the Diocese of Los Angeles, it was designed by his son, architect Reginald D. Johnson. The chapel served as St. Alban's Church until 1941, when a church adjacent to the chapel was completed. P.P. Lewis was the architect for the new church building.

St. Alban's whitewashed walls and dark woodwork are illumined by the stained glass windows created by Judson Studios. The 25 windows in the church, and eight in the chapel, are all memorials or gifts. The windows on the north side of the nave commemorate significant events and individuals in Biblical and church history, such as the conversion of St. Paul, the Annunciation, and the trial of St. Alban. Several others celebrate the English roots of the Episcopal church, including the Magna Carta and English prayer book windows.

Most of the clerestory windows illustrate the book of Revelation. The number seven figures prominently in their design, a reference to the letters to the seven churches cited in Revelation.

Being built to serve the students at UCLA, the chapel includes several windows which refer to higher education and professional accomplishment. Added over the years since the chapel was built in 1931, these windows include an image of a stained-glass astronaut indicating expanded knowledge of the universe, and a Professions window celebrating the fields of law, medicine, accounting and writing. Jesus explaining to Nicodemus the concept of being born again, and teaching the multitudes from a boat on the Lake of Gennesaret are the central subjects of the Teaching window.

Shields in the window honor education in Southern California

The baptistery window illustrates Christ welcoming all children

SUFFER THE LITTLE CHILDREN

The transom window shows scenes from the life of Jesus

The altar, carved with saints and martyrs

OPPOSITE PAGE: The church was built to meet the spiritual needs of UCLA students and faculty

The baptismal font

ST. ANDREW CATHOLIC CHURCH

St. Andrew Catholic Church, Pasadena

RIGHT: The Stations of the Cross and scenes from the life of Christ are painted above the columns

OPPOSITE PAGE: The multi-colored columns are scagliola work, a means of replicating marble

Detail of the chapel tabernacle

By the year 1886, there were an estimated 400 Catholics living in Pasadena, all of whom had to travel to Los Angeles or the San Gabriel Mission to attend Mass. A proposal to the Bishop of Los Angeles resulted in the creation of the first parish in Pasadena that same year. Early parishioners attended services in a hotel and a public school, and eventually a frame church was built on corner of Pasadena Avenue and Bellefontaine Street and named St. Andrew. When a larger edifice was needed, the congregation relocated to the northeast corner of Walnut and Fair Oaks avenues.

The current St. Andrew church was built in 1927 in Romanesque style. It was designed by Ross Montgomery, who took as his inspiration two churches in Rome. The façade and campanile of St. Andrew are replicas of the 12th century Santa Maria in Cosmedin; its interior recalls the Basilica of Santa Sabina.

The 24 Corinthian columns which line the Sanctuary are stucco, marbelized by a 17th century technique known as scagliola, in which gypsum, glue and marble dust coat the columns and are polished to a high sheen.

A series of murals by Italian artist Carlo Wostry, who also created art work for the Church of the Blessed Sacrament in Hollywood, illustrates episodes from the life of St. Andrew, the church's namesake. St. Andrew with John the Baptist, at the marriage feast at Cana and baptizing in the Jordan River are among the subjects of the murals, painted in one-dimensional, semi-Byzantine style. Wostry also painted Stations of the Cross as well as the huge interpretation of God the Creator and Jesus and the disciples over the altar. In the chapel of All Saints, Wostry illustrated St. Michael and archangels Gabriel and Raphael. Below them is the Madonna on a throne, surrounded by saints and angels.

Three stained glass windows in the baptistery show Christ being baptized by St. John, the baptism of St. Paul, and St. Patrick baptizing the High King of Ireland in the year 432. Along the south wall of the baptistery is a symbolic retelling of the fall of man and his regeneration.

The domed ceiling of the baptistery

OPPOSITE PAGE: The mural above the high altar is in the style of the early Christian church, showing God the Creator over Jesus and the twelve apostles

The painted ceiling in the narthex

Italian artist, Carlos Wostry painted the murals for St. Andrew in the 1930s

TOP AND ABOVE: Paintings of saints in the All Saints' Chapel

The altar in The Blessed Sacrament Chapel

OPPOSITE PAGE: Looking through the baptistery gates into the narthex

BELOW FAR RIGHT: The baptismal font

Details of the church's painted ceilings

ST. BRENDAN CATHOLIC CHURCH

St. Brendan Catholic Church, Los Angeles

A large carved wood crucifix in the narthex of St. Brendan

A stone fountain in the courtyard of the church

OPPOSITE PAGE: The golden tabernacle in front of the reredos contains the elements of the Host

French Gothic architecture inspired the design for St. Brendan Catholic Church, whose architect was Emmet G. Martin. Midnight Mass on Christmas Eve, 1927, was the first service held in the church, and was celebrated by Fr. William Forde. In 1915, this young Irish priest had been sent to Los Angeles by the Vicar General of the Diocese of Monterey-Los Angeles, who appointed him the pastor of an enormous parish in what was then a primarily residential area of Los Angeles. Fr. Forde oversaw the construction of a one-room church attached to a parochial school on Western Avenue, and named them both after St. Brendan, a sixth-century Irish explorer and builder of monasteries throughout Ireland and Wales.

By the 1920s, the establishment of additional Catholic churches in the area reconfigured the boundaries of Fr. Forde's parish. The location for the new church was west of the old one, at Third Street and Van Ness Avenue.

Complementing the Caen and Boise stone ornamentation on the interior of the building are the large American oak carvings by Belgian artist Martin Barbier. These are set in niches along the north aisle of the Sanctuary and show scenes from the life of Jesus. The stained glass windows, from the German studio of Dr. Gerhard Oidtmann, were shipped in panels and reassembled on site.

Members of the congregation underwrote the cost of numerous elements of the church, including the Mary Altar and the tower bells. Parishioners who owned lumber companies donated pews and doors. Much of the ornamental and baptistery ironwork was hand-forged by the Campbell Ironworks, a business owned by the family of Sr. Albertine, who taught at St. Brendan's School for more than a decade.

During the 1940s-1950s, much of the interior of St. Brendan was refurbished under the direction of Fr. Thomas Fogarty. New statuary and three major new altars were among the refinements added to the church at this time. In the early 1990s, the baptismal font was moved from the chapel to the steps of the Sanctuary. The church gardens and south patio were re-landscaped in 2001.

A carved and painted arch of the wooden vaulted Sanctuary ceiling

OPPOSITE PAGE: The crucifixion figure over the altar is carved of white oak and hung against a reredos of golden mosaic

Carved oak vignettes from the life of Jesus, along the north aisle of the Sanctuary, were created by Belgian artist Martin Barbier

"If your sins be as scarlet, they shall be made as white as snow."

Isaias : 15 . 7.

The stained glass windows, from the Gerhard Oidtmann studios in Germany, are signed, an unusual detail. They illustrate scenes from the life of Jesus.

Baldacchino over the altar crucifix is of polished bronze and French glass

LEFT: The beautiful handpainted ceiling in the narthex of the church

The carved stone baptismal font

RIGHT: A 1979 painting from the Arthur Hercz Studio

FAR RIGHT: One of the ironwork chandeliers original to the church

ST. JAMES' EPISCOPAL CHURCH

St. James' Episcopal Church, Los Angeles

Christ blesses his followers

The cornerstone

Ⅰn 1912, the total monthly parish income for St. James' Episcopal Church was $12, contributed by the membership of sixteen. Within four years, the church, at the corner of Ardmore Avenue and Pico Boulevard, had increased its membership to 250. Moving into a Craftsman-style house at Western Avenue and Monette Place met the church's needs until 1920, when, at a cost of $1,175, the church was physically moved to Wilshire Boulevard and St. Andrews Place. Four years later Benjamin McDougall was named architect for the present church building.

In 1995, the 1911 Murray Harris organ from St. Paul's Episcopal Cathedral, which had been demolished in 1980, was installed in St. James'. Named after the late organist and choirmaster of St. James' who spearheaded the acquisition project, the David John Falconer Memorial Organ was placed in the front of the church, with decorative cases of red oak added to accommodate the organ chambers.

The stained glass windows along the north side of the church showcase the sacraments of the Episcopal Church. Those along the south side illustrate episodes and parables from the life of Jesus, including his temptations in the wilderness and the story of the Good Samaritan.

Other artifacts reclaimed from St. Paul's, including chandeliers and wood paneling, are found in the Columbarium Chapel, a repository for the ashes of cremated parishioners. Church decorator Rhett Judice painted the murals of angels, while light streams through a stained glass window symbolizing the Holy Spirit.

Details of the Gothic-style woodwork

The pulpit

The lectern

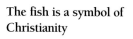

The fish is a symbol of
Christianity

The baptismal font

The tile floors include
Christian symbolism

ST. JAMES' EPISCOPAL CHURCH

The church was designed in 1924 by Benjamin McDougall

The David John Falconer Memorial Organ incorporates portions of the instrument originally built for the old St. Paul's Cathedral

Much of the chapel's woodwork is from the old St. Paul's Cathedral

TOP LEFT: Christ and symbols of his power above the chapel altar

OPPOSITE PAGE, LEFT, AND BELOW:
The paintings of angels in the Columbarium Chapel are by Rhett Judice

Votives in the chapel

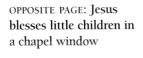

The sacraments of the Episcopal Church are the theme of the windows along the north side of the church

OPPOSITE PAGE: Jesus blesses little children in a chapel window

The stained glass windows at St. James' were created by Judson Studios

SAINT JOHN'S EPISCOPAL CHURCH

St. John's Episcopal Church, Los Angeles

OPPOSITE PAGE: **Eight columns support the octagonal bowl of the baptismal font; eight is considered the number of new life. The font is carved with symbols of the trinity.**

Angels protect the Holy Family in the windows of the south transept.

Although it is built primarily of reinforced concrete, the exterior of the church was inspired by the 11th century stone Church of San Pietro, outside Rome. Under the direction of Cartiano Scarpitta, a team of Italian sculptors fashioned the columns, bas reliefs around the rose window, and other exterior sculptures. Scarpitta used his younger son as a model for the sculpture of St. John the Evangelist which decorates the Carrara marble lectern, used for reading Bible lessons.

The Davis brothers designed the wooden ceiling of the church's interior after another Italian Romanesque church, San Mineato al Monte in Florence. Following the traditional custom of honoring the church's patron in its art work, the image of Dr. George Davidson, rector of St. John's during its construction and dedication, was painted on one of huge ceiling beams of Oregon pine. The life-sized crucifix on the rood beam, and the triptych above the high altar were carved by Adelbert Zwink.

The 10 windows lining the aisles represent scenes from the life of Christ. A mosaic at the east end of the nave portrays the Transfiguration: the disciples Peter, James and John observing the meeting of Moses, Jesus and Elijah. Among the Biblical prophets and saints represented in the clerestory windows on the south side of the nave is a representation of Dr. Martin Luther King, Jr., honored as a martyr. The central altar of St. John's was designed by J. Todd Campbell, a member of the congregation, in 1967.

A wood-shingled, Gothic Revival-style building in an orange grove was the first St. John's Episcopal Church, built in 1890, the same year the congregation was organized. After the end of World War I, the membership had grown to such an extent that a design competition was held for a new building to be constructed on the same site. The winning design, for a northern Italian Romanesque-style structure, was submitted by Pierpont and Walter Davis, brothers who later designed apartment buildings throughout Los Angeles. Construction on the new St. John's began in 1922; the church was consecrated three years later.

Along the south side of the church, mosaic angels sing and play music

Varied colors of marble in the columns of the altar kneeling rail

The risen Christ, above the altar, is surrounded by early saints of the Christian church.

Carved marble surrounds the golden door of the tabernacle

OPPOSITE PAGE: The arcade of ten arches supported by ten columns refers to the Ten Commandments

152

SAINT JOHN'S EPISCOPAL CHURCH

Scarpitta, the sculptor of the marble lectern, used his son as the model for St. John

The chapel was decorated in 1968 with Byzantine-style mosaics by Derrick John Taylor and artists from Judson Studios

The dome of the apse is decorated with a triangle inside a trefoil – symbols of the Trinity. The angles of the triangle point to Latin words for "father," "son," and "holy spirit"

OPPOSITE PAGE: The rood beam, containing the life-sized crucifix, is painted with the words "He was wounded for our transgressions."

A clerestory window shows Martin Luther King, Jr.

ST. MARK'S EPISCOPAL CHURCH

St. Mark's Episcopal Church, Glendale

RIGHT: Mosaic at the main
entrance to the church

OPPOSITE PAGE: The baptismal
font from the 1914 St. Mark's

All of the memorial
windows in the church
were executed by
Judson Studios

TO THE LAND FORCES OF THE UNITED STATES

The first Episcopal bishop of California, Bishop William Kip, authorized the Mission of the Good Shepherd in March, 1889. After several years of services in private homes and, later, in an Episcopal girls' school, the congregation built its first church at Broadway and Isabel streets in Glendale in 1893. The following year, at the annual convention of the Diocese of California, the mission was granted a name change, to St. Mark's Mission, Glendale. In 1914, in addition to moving to a new building at Harvard and Louise streets, the church was incorporated as the Parish Church of St. Mark, Glendale.

By the end of World War II, with the city expanding north towards the Verdugo mountains, the members of St. Mark's selected the southeast corner of Brand Boulevard and Dryden Street as the site for a new church. Architect Carleton M. Winslow designed a Gothic-style building of poured concrete, which was finished in 1948 in time for Christmas Eve services. With snow falling, the congregation carried candles outside the church for its dedication on Epiphany, 1949.

From the prior St. Mark's church came the baptismal font and the chapel altar. A tapestry hanging of angels originally hung in the Episcopal Cathedral of St. Paul, which was closed in 1979 and later demolished due to seismic and safety considerations. Within the past few years, the altar area and ceiling were redesigned and painted by church architect and decorator Rhett Judice. The enamel tabernacle showing the Lamb of God was created by Jerry Campbell.

Judson Studios executed the stained glass windows of St. Mark's. The chapel windows on the south side of the nave are dedicated to the Land, Sea and Air forces of World War II. The theme of the southern clerestory windows is "The Earthly Life of Our Lord," and includes illustrations of the Annunciation, the Nativity, Jesus as a child, in the temple, and being baptized, the Sermon on the Mount, and the Transfiguration, among others. The north side windows include scenes of Christian healing, the parables of the Good Samaritan and the Prodigal Son, the Last Supper and the Crucifixion.

The Gothic-style church seats approximately 450

OPPOSITE PAGE: The Te Deum window above the high altar features Christ Enthroned in the top center panel, surrounded by saints and archbishops of the Anglican church

Contemporary church architect and designer Rhett Judice redesigned the chancel and altar paintings at St. Mark's

The light in the Sanctuary lamp symbolizes the presence of the Holy Spirit

St. Mary of the Angels Anglican Church

St. Mary of the Angels Anglican Church, Hollywood

RIGHT: A statue of the church's namesake in the courtyard

OPPOSITE PAGE: The seven lamps above the Sanctuary represent the seven gifts of the Holy Spirit

A detail at the entrance

At a time when few churches welcomed actors as members, St. Mary of the Angels, founded in 1919, began as a mission to address the spiritual needs of Anglo-Catholic performers in the new motion picture industry. Fr. Neal Dodd, the founding rector, eventually became a technical advisor on correct liturgical procedure for the film studios.

Originally the church building was conceived as a chapel which would serve a basilica planned for the site and surrounding acreage. The Depression intervened, funding was not available, and the church's building plans were never realized.

The spectacular altar pieces, original 16th century Della Robbia faience from Florence, is one of only three such sets in existence; the other two are in Italy and England. The glazed terra cotta figures of the Annunciation, St. John and St. Francis, and a pair of urns, were gifts to Fr. Dodd from the founder of the May Company department stores in the 1920s. Originally installed in the church courtyard, they were moved inside to protect them from the damaging effects of smog.

Also from Italy are the carved wooden panels showing the Stations of the Cross and a crucifix on the south wall of the church. The seven lamps hanging above the altar represent the seven gifts of the Holy Ghost, and the cross above the altar is known as a rood cross, named after the medieval English term for the beam across the chancel of the church. Figures from St. Mary's original altar screens have been incorporated into the wooden pulpit.

The clerestory windows illustrate English saints, while the lower windows represent the sacraments of baptism, marriage, etc. A more recent addition to the church, and a tribute to St. Mary's original outreach, is a large circular stained glass window of St. Genesius, patron saint of actors, created by Judson Studios. In one hand the saint holds a hook, in the other an actor's mask.

A plaque represents the shield of the Anglican Church

Judson Studios used English glass for the St. Genesius window

An icon
in a side chapel

OPPOSITE PAGE: The 16th century
Della Robbia altarpiece

St. George slays his dragon

LEFT: One of the two Della Robbia urns
which complement the altarpiece

St. Matthew's Parish Church

St. Matthew's Parish Church, Pacific Palisades

Looking up from under the bell tower

A bronze fountain in the church's garden

There was an unusual requirement in the contract between St. Matthew's Parish and the architectural firm of Moore Ruble Yudell: the final design for the parish's new Episcopal church in Pacific Palisades would have to be approved by two-thirds of the 350-member congregation.

For Charles W. Moore, principle in the firm, the solution was self-evident: the membership would design the church.

St. Matthew's Parish began in 1940, when six Episcopalian women started holding services, first in a library in Temescal Canyon, and then in private homes. The first St. Matthew's Church was built in 1942 on Swarthmore Avenue in Pacific Palisades, and was later moved to Bienveneda Avenue. Fire destroyed the building in the late 1970s.

Moore and his partners hosted four, all-day design workshops for the parishioners of St. Matthew's. At the first session, participants were given collage materials ranging from cellophane to breakfast cereal and told to construct their vision of the new church. At the next workshop, the architects supplied models of pews, altars, bell towers, and other components of a church, and when each group of workshop attendees had completed its design, the architects were delighted to see that everyone agreed on the same basic layout: a half-circle of pews around the altar. As Moore Ruble Yudell drew up plans incorporating the wishes of the members, the firm also welcomed input from the parishioners on the shape of the roof and the building's siting.

Of particular concern were the acoustics of the church, as plans included a 36-foot-high organ. Moore Rubel Yudell solved the debate between those who recognized the acoustical need for hard plaster wall surfaces, and the members who wanted wood used extensively, as a reference to their former church. The architects' solution was a pattern of deep wood battens against plaster walls painted in shades chosen to harmonize with the natural shades of the wood.

When the final plans for the church were presented to the St. Matthew's congregation, 83 percent of the votes cast were in favor of the design. After four years of planning, designing and construction, the church was completed in 1983.

RIGHT: A crucifix above the altar of the chapel

OPPOSITE PAGE: The organ's design is influenced by the Arts and Crafts Movement

Water from the baptismal font circulates back to the garden

RIGHT: Parishioners requested semi-circular seating around the altar

The door of the Tabernacle in the Chapel depicts wheat and grapes, symbols of bread and wine of the Holy Eucharist

The Chapel opens to the left of adjacent Sanctuary

St. Monica Catholic Church

St. Monica Catholic Church, Santa Monica

RIGHT: **Corinthian columns are featured throughout the church**

FAR RIGHT: **A shrine to St. Therese in the vestibule**

OPPOSITE PAGE: **Rays from the Holy Spirit reach Mary, St. Joseph, and the risen Christ**

Both the parish, established in 1886, and the city of Santa Monica itself were named for the mother of St. Augustine, whose prayers for her dissolute son resulted in his conversion and dedication to the Catholic Church.

As with St. Andrew's Roman Catholic Church in Pasadena, the Basilica of Santa Sabina in Rome was the inspiration for the interior of St. Monica Catholic Church. Architect A.C. Martin completed the church, at a reported cost of $340,000, in time for its Christmas services in 1925.

The granite statues and detail work on the exterior of the building were sculpted by Joseph Conradi. Corinthian columns line the nave, supporting the barrel-vaulted ceiling. The narthex of the church contains shrines to St. Joseph and St. Therese. The five joyful, five sorrowful and five glorious mysteries of the rosary are the theme of the clerestory stained glass windows. Three more windows illustrate St. Dominic, St. Patrick and Mary holding her crucified Son.

The Stations of the Cross are rendered in marble and mosaic tile along the side aisle walls of the church. Comparable tiles decorate the baptismal font, pulpit, and altar, which includes a bas-relief of the Last Supper. The stained glass windows above the Stations illustrate the eleven disciples, minus Judas. A Resurrection mural fills the dome above the altar, showing the risen Christ with Mary and St. Joseph. Prominent are the Greek letters alpha and omega, signifying that Christ is the beginning and the end. The altar table encloses relics of Fr. Junipero Serra, St. Augustine, and St. Monica. At the front of the church are murals showing St. Monica, garbed in blue, her son St. Augustine, and the four evangelists, each with his symbol.

The church suffered massive damage in the Northridge earthquake of 1994. After more than a year of restoration, rebuilding and some rearranging, St. Monica again opened its doors for services in 1995.

The choir loft houses the 1300-pipe organ

Votive lights in the shrine of the Sacred Heart of Jesus

The pulpit is inlaid with black and white marble

St. Monica rendered in Byzantine style

OPPOSITE PAGE: The three marble figures at the top of the altar represent Faith, Charity and Hope

The shrine of the Blessed Virgin Mary

The altar table includes relics of
Fr. Junipero Serra, St. Augustine,
and St. Monica

The Eucharistic Reservation
area contains the tabernacle

The
tabernacle
is decorated
with the
Alpha and
Omega
(beginning
and end)
symbols

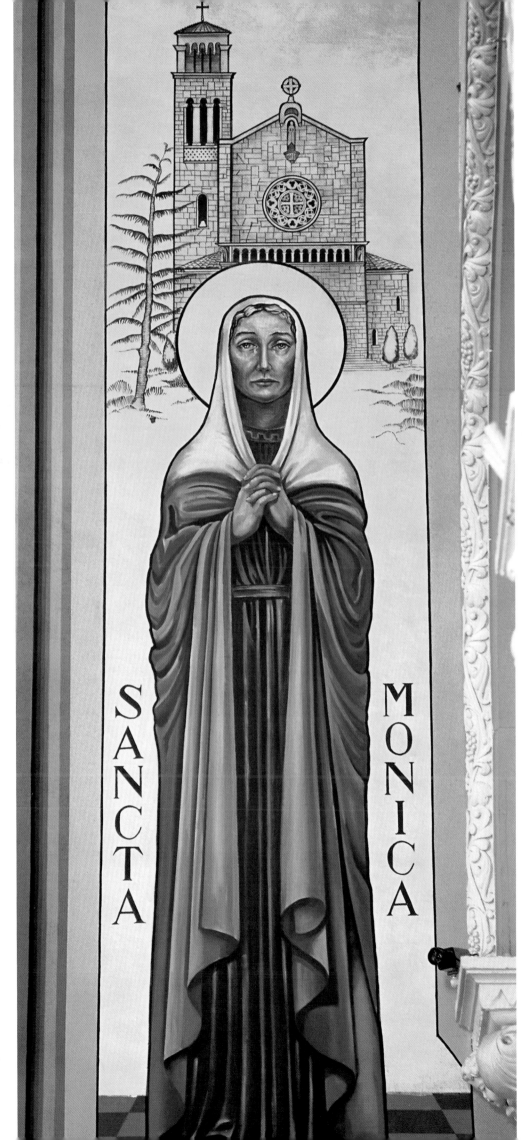

St. Monica in stained glass

A mural of St. Monica

Mosaic detail

The shrine of the Sacred Heart of Jesus

St. Nicholas Antiochian Orthodox Cathedral

St. Nicholas Antiochian Orthodox Cathedral, Los Angeles

RIGHT: The chalice, Gospel and the top of the baptismal font

OPPOSITE PAGE: Icon of St. George in the St. George Chapel where baptisms are held. The chapel was added in 1976

Although attempts to establish an Antiochian church in Los Angeles had begun at the turn of the 20th century, it wasn't until 1924 that Americans of Arabic descent united for services at St. George Orthodox Church, a four-room bungalow at 36th Street and Gramercy Place.

By 1943, the Orthodox community numbered 350 families, and the newly formed St. Nicholas Orthodox Society addressed the need to establish a larger house of worship in Los Angeles. Eventually land was purchased on Third Street and Paul R. Williams, who designed numerous well known residences and commercial buildings throughout Southern California, was hired as church architect. The cornerstone was laid in 1948 and the church was completed in 1950 at a cost of $600,000.

Artist Innocenzo Dario executed most of the original artwork and Icons in St. Nicholas. The Byzantine Icons were written by Nicholas Majdalani. The traditional panocrator Icon in the dome depicts Christ as God Almighty surrounded by the four evangelists. On the cathedral's west wall, subjects of the Icons include Elijah ascending to heaven observed by his successor Elisha; St. Paul preaching in Athens; Maloola, saint of the St. Takla convent, and Moses receiving the Ten Commandments. The stained glass windows on the same wall represent saints Gabriel, Nicholas, and Michael. Icons in the west balcony are of the Annunciation and the Salutation of Mary by her cousin Elizabeth.

The altar iconostasis includes the figures of Mary and Jesus, John the Baptist, St. Nicholas, and archangels Gabriel and Michael rendered in mosaic tile. These mosaics were manufactured in Florence, Italy, by the 500-year-old firm of Michael Mellini. In 1980, Dario was commissioned to paint a panoramic Icon of Jerusalem at the time of Christ. It is behind the altar. The figures in the Icons on the pulpit are the authors of the Orthodox Liturgy.

The huge baptismal font is located in the St. George Chapel in the south transept of the cathedral. An Icon of St. Nicholas towers over the door to this chapel, which was added to the church in 1976.

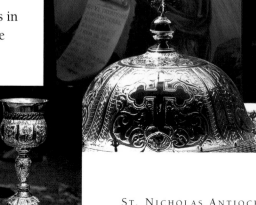

The Parthenos, the enormous Icon of the Virgin and Child over the altar, welcomes, blesses and protects the faithful

FAR LEFT: Figures in the Icons on the pulpit are the authors of the Orthodox Liturgy

LEFT: The altar table

The mosaic figures in the iconostasis were created in Florence, Italy

Christ enters Jerusalem

ST. GABRIEL   ST. NICHOLAS   ST. MICHAEL

Wise men honor the Christ-child

OPPOSITE PAGE: The west wall window show
St. Gabriel, St. Nicholas and St. Michael

Detail of
the chapel
tabernacle

Most of the paintings were executed
by Innocenzo Dario

RIGHT: Daily services
are held in this chapel

ST. TIMOTHY CATHOLIC CHURCH

St. Timothy Church, Los Angeles

OPPOSITE PAGE: **The tabernacle was crafted in the special effects department of MGM studios**

RIGHT: **Wrought iron cherubs decorate the altar rail**

Founded in 1943, St. Timothy's parish originally held services first in a store front on Pico Boulevard, and later in what is now the parish hall. On Christmas, 1949, the doors were opened for Mass in the newly completed church, which was designed by architect Harold Gimeno.

The Spanish altarpiece was originally intended for a church in Mexico being built in the early 1900s. Confiscated by the Mexican government and sold to a New York art dealer, the altar was eventually purchased by the wife of a Doheny oil executive in Los Angeles who intended to install it in a new Episcopalian church she planned to sponsor. Upon her death, with her church still not built, her heirs placed the altar up for auction in the early 1940s, when representatives of St.

Timothy's successfully bid for it. Two painted panels were removed from the main altar for use as focal points for the two side altars.

With several devoted parishioners employed in prominent positions in the art departments of Twentieth Century Fox and MGM studios, much of the décor of St. Timothy's has a cinematic provenance. The statues of the Virgin Mary and St. Joseph at the two side altars were purchased from Twentieth Century Fox, after being featured in the set of "St. Mary's Home for Boys" in "The Jolson Story." Under the direction of a St. Timothy's parishioner, the church's tabernacle was designed and executed by craftsmen at MGM. Constructed of gold-plated brass, it is decorated with silver figures of the 12 apostles.

A strike at the Fox studios had beneficial consequences for the church: with its woodshop carpenters officially on strike, the studio allowed its employees to join St. Timothy's members to build pews for the church at the studio. Several of the paintings in the nave were painted by Thomas Lawless, an assistant art director for MGM who later painted religious subjects. His paintings include a stylized portrait of the church's namesake, St. Timothy, companion of St. Paul, who was later named Bishop of Ephesus. Lawless also copied Raphael's Transfiguration and Sistine Madonna for St. Timothy's.

The side altar dedicated to Virgin Mary

The main altarpiece is Spanish; its date and provenance are not known

The base of the pulpit came from the William Randolph Hearst collection

This painting of the Madonna and Child, and St. Lawrence and St. Francis, is thought to be a copy of one by 16th century artist Monenico Campagnola

St. Anthony atop the altar

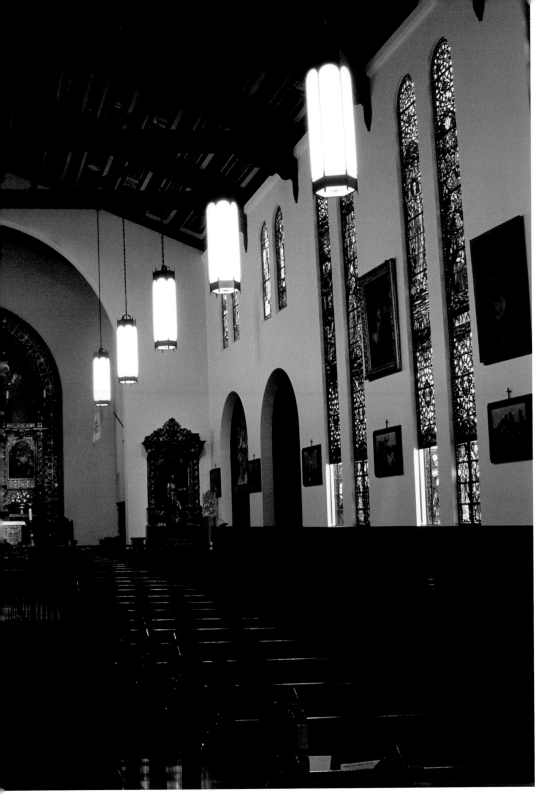

The shrine to St. Joseph

"The Presentation of the Child Jesus in the Temple" is thought to be from the 17th century

A detail of an altar candlestick

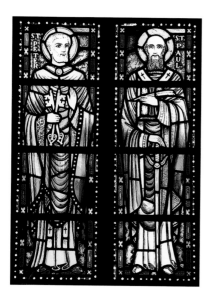
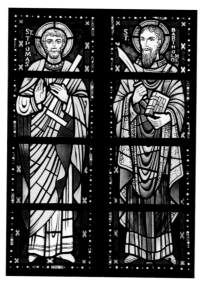

The rose window includes the symbols of the four evangelists

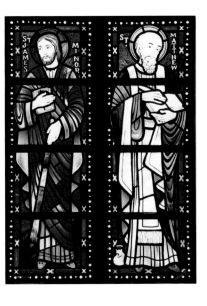

St. Timothy's has 67 stained glass windows, many representing saints and Biblical figures

The organ loft

St. Elizabeth
Ann Seton

St. Augustine,
Bishop of Hippo, with
his "Confessions"

Baptistery statues include St. Anthony, St. Ann and child Mary, the Sacred Heart of Jesus, and St. Elizabeth Ann Seton

The entrance to the baptistery

A copy of a painting of St. Timothy, painted by Thomas Lawless

OPPOSITE PAGE: A cross etched in the baptistery window

Details of the floor and wall tiles throughout the church

ST. VINCENT DE PAUL
ROMAN CATHOLIC CHURCH

St. Vincent de Paul Roman
Catholic Church, Los Angeles

obscure the beauty of the church, including its elaborately tiled dome. Although the Spanish Churrigueresque style of Mexican cathedrals was Martin's inspiration for the design of the building, constructed in the shape of a Latin cross, many of the interior details are European.

The carved and polychrome wood reredos, the background for the main altar, includes paintings of Greek and Latin Fathers of the Church, the twelve apostles, and other church figures significant to St. Vincent's. The Stations of the Cross are devised of gilt and colored mosaic on the pillars lining the Sanctuary. The eight paintings in the dome, which is 45 feet in diameter, represent the four evangelists and their symbols. John Smeraldi of Pasadena executed these paintings, as well as the highly decorative ceiling motifs.

Paneled in French walnut, the baptistery includes a black marble font crowned with a canopy of bronze. In this area are housed relics of St. Vincent de Paul and Francis Regis Clet, a Vincentian priest martyred in China, among others.

The stained glass windows in the church were all designed by Wilbur H. Burnham and Harry W. Goodhue of Boston. The six stained glass windows of the Sanctuary feature six angels holding plaques bearing the symbols of six sacraments, the altar representing the seventh. The theme of the window over the entrance to St. Vincent's is the Resurrection, and illustrates Jesus between an angel and a Roman soldier. At the base of these figures is Archangel Michael standing victorious over Satan. The smaller aisle windows illustrate episodes from the life of St. Vincent de Paul.

RIGHT: A detail of the organ console screen

OPPOSITE PAGE: **The dome paintings represent the four evangelists and their symbols**

Named after the 16th century French Apostle of Charity, the St. Vincent de Paul parish in Los Angeles began in 1887, when Roman Catholic worshippers met for Mass in the chapel of St. Vincent's College at Washington Boulevard and Grand Avenue. Within the next 30 years, the area had become so densely populated that in October 1923, ground was broken for a church that would accommodate 1200.

Architect Albert C. Martin set the building on a 45-degree axis to both Adams and Figueroa streets, ensuring that no commercial development would ever

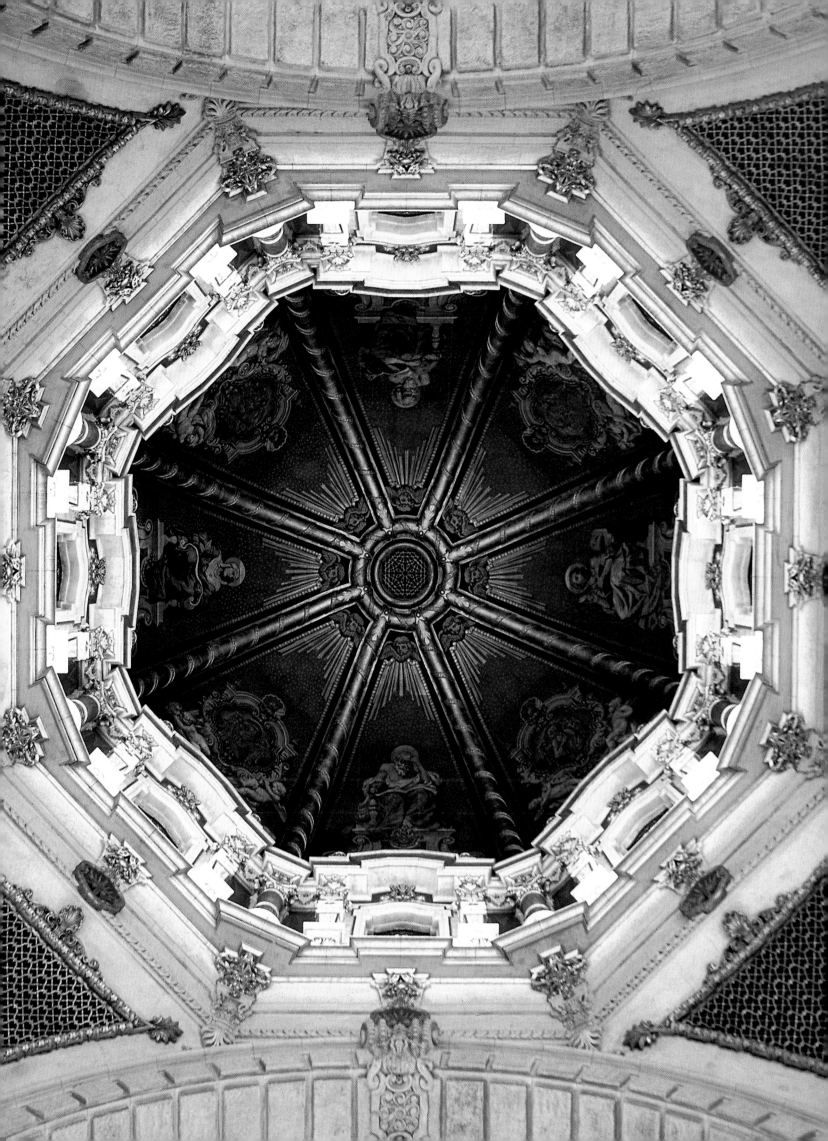

The Stations of the Cross are rendered in mosaic

Statues of saints and Vincentian martyrs in the base of the reredos

The central panel of the Crucifixion in the reredos is flanked by paintings of four Greek Fathers of the Church on the left, and four Latin Fathers of the Church on the right

One of the clerestory windows commemorating the miracles of Jesus

The ceiling is painted with symbols of Christianity

The pulpit is carved of red Moroccan marble, with a canopy of French walnut

Shrines are in the Spanish Churrigueresque style

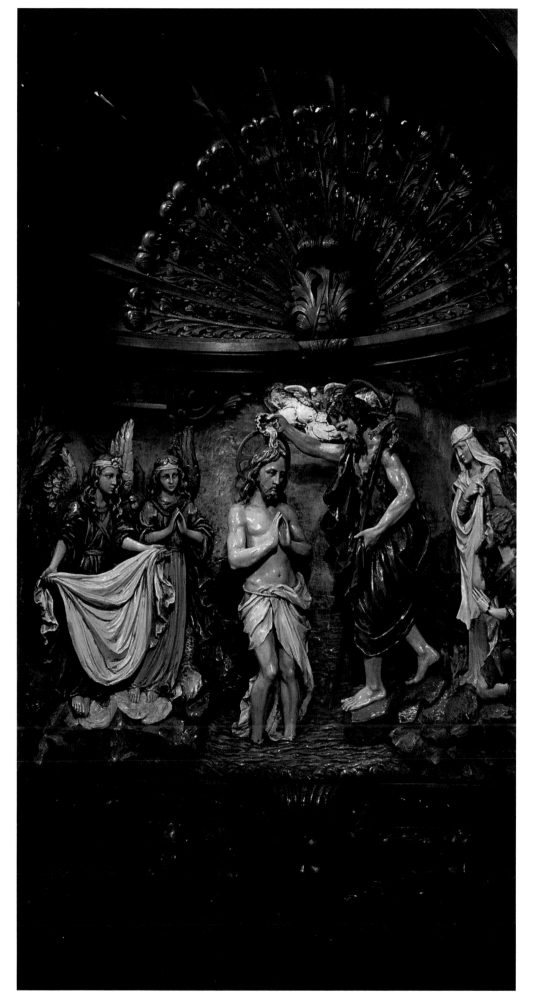

Numerous relics are kept
in the baptistery

Detail of baptistery carving

OPPOSITE PAGE: The black marble
baptismal font is surrounded by
walls of French walnut

A polychrome wood panel illustrates
Christ's baptism by John the Baptist

A relic of St. Vincent de Paul is within
this small elaborately decorated case

THE CATHEDRAL CENTER OF ST. PAUL
(EPISCOPAL)

The Cathedral Center of St. Paul, Los Angeles

Named after a fourth-century bishop of Alexandria, St. Athanasius Episcopal Church began in 1864 in downtown Los Angeles. As membership grew, the parish renamed itself St. Paul's, and in 1889 built a Victorian Gothic church on the site of the current Biltmore Hotel. Some members who preferred a smaller church re-claimed the name St. Athanasius and formed a subsequent congregation. In the early 1920s, St. Paul's went on to build St. Paul's Cathedral at Wilshire Boulevard and Figueroa Street. St. Athanasius built a church on Custer Street in 1902, and then, in 1919, with the gift of property on Echo Park Avenue, cut its building in half to facilitate its move to Echo Park.

After the 1979 earthquake, St. Paul's Cathedral was demolished and the two parishes voted to merge. Eventually, the Echo Park site of St. Athanasius was selected as the right neighborhood for a new Cathedral Center, which would incorporate not only the administrative offices for the diocese, but appropriate space for the church's ministries, such as health care, housing, youth and community development programs. Completed in 1994, the Center's 102,000-square-foot complex was designed by architect John Andre Gougeon.

At the heart of the Center is the church. Several items of furniture from old St. Paul's Cathedral were installed in the new church, including the Bishop's, Dean's and Suffragan Bishop's chairs and the baptismal font.

Altarware for the sacrament of the Eucharist

OPPOSITE PAGE: The church's flexible seating can accommodate more than 500

The church was designed by John Andre Gougeon

The Bishop's Cathedra, from old St. Paul's Cathedral

The altar (above) and stained glass window (right) in the Lazarus Chapel are from St. Athanasius Church

FAR LEFT: The Suffragan Bishop's chair

OPPOSITE PAGE: The candlesticks and eagle lectern are from old St. Paul's Cathedral

The baptismal font

The shield of the first bishop of Los
Angeles, Joseph Horsfall Johnson

A 17th century chest from old
St. Paul's Cathedral

The aumbrey holds the Reserve Sacrament
after the Eucharist

The shield of the
Episcopal Diocese
of Los Angeles

The ambo
(moveable pulpit)

OPPOSITE PAGE: Our
Lady of Guadalupe
198

THE CATHEDRAL OF ST. SOPHIA

St. Sophia Greek Orthodox
Cathedral, Los Angeles

A detail of the carved
oak entry portals

Detail of the main
entrance to the
cathedral

and George, had parlayed the money they had earned as waiters in their new country into an empire of film production and distribution and theater construction. Spyros eventually became the president of Twentieth Century Fox. George was the president and chairman of United Artists Theaters on the East Coast. Charles, who had a particular interest in theater building, was president of National Theaters and Fox West Coast Theaters.

A Byzantine cross

Charles P. Skouras had no intention of building another village church. For his inspiration he chose the Hagia Sophia, the Cathedral of the Holy Wisdom of God, built by the Emperor Justinian in Constantinople between 532 and 537. As architect, he chose Gus Kalionzes. Although World War II interrupted Skouras' construction plans, groundbreaking for the new 900-seat cathedral took place in July 1948, and St. Sophia was dedicated four years later.

Skouras selected a fellow Greek, William Chavalas, to serve as the master artist who would oversee the ornamental plasterers, gilders, artisans and painters, many of whom had decorated Skouras Theaters across the country, in their new assignment at St. Sophia. Chavalas and his team completed much of the painting in a warehouse studio in Culver City and later installed it within the church. Skouras gave Chavalas creative leeway with the iconography in the church; it is a modification of the traditional style, incorporating elements more identifiable as Italian Renaissance than strict Byzantine.

By the 1940s, the Greek community in Los Angeles had outgrown its original house of worship, the Annunciation, on San Julian Street. Built in 1912, it was a small building reminiscent of the churches found in Greek villages. Film mogul Charles P. Skouras presented the Greek Orthodox Church membership, which then numbered approximately 1,000, with an unorthodox offer: he would raise the necessary funds for a magnificent new cathedral, build it, and turn it over to the church community debt-free on the condition that he alone would oversee its design and execution.

Upon emigrating from Greece in the first decade of the 20th century, Charles P. Skouras, along with his brothers Spyros

OPPOSITE PAGE: A stained glass window of
St. John towers above the altar table

The massive chandeliers are Czechoslovakian crystal

LEFT: The baptismal font was designed by William Chavalas and is made of gold-plated bronze

FAR LEFT: The dome portrait of Christ as Lord of All is executed in mosaic

Byzantine-inspired mosaic recurs throughout St. Sophia

Bird iconography includes the phoenix, symbol of the Resurrection, the dove, sign of the Holy Spirit, and the owl, ancient representative of wisdom

God's Justice is the theme of a panel painting along the back wall of the cathedral

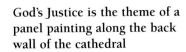

The iconostasion, or icon screen, separates the east end of the nave from the altar

ABOVE: The cast-stone pulpit is decorated in gold leaf

RIGHT: Archangel Michael guards the iconostasion

CENTER: The phoenix, symbol of the Resurrection, surmounts each gate to the altar table

The mural above the choir loft shows the prophet Elijah ascending to heaven in a flaming chariot

Christ greets His congregation from the right side of the iconostasion

Madonna and Child in a niche in the iconostasion

LEFT: The Resurrection of Christ is the theme of the trilogy of paintings on the south transept

RIGHT: Lions guard the Bishop's Throne, reserved for Christ's representative on earth

BELOW: A detail of the Bishop's chair; the eagle symbolizes the authority of Christ

A gilded Gospel

THE CATHEDRAL OF ST. SOPHIA

The interior of
Charles P.
Skouras' crypt

LEFT: The Skouras
mausoleum is on
the grounds of St.
Sophia

Detail of the door to
the crypt

OPPOSITE PAGE:
Windows along
the north and
south walls of the
nave illustrate
the twelve
apostles

TRINITY BAPTIST CHURCH

Trinity Baptist Church, Santa Monica

OPPOSITE PAGE: **American symbols of freedom and independence are represented, along with images of Jesus, John and other evangelists, and St. Francis.**

The colors of the rose window are unusual; typically they are reds and blues

I n November of 1924, in order to meet the need for a Baptist church in northern Santa Monica, 87 members from Immanuel Baptist and First Baptist churches convened to organize what would become Trinity Baptist Church. Its first service was held in January of the following year, in the Masonic Temple at Santa Monica Boulevard and Tenth Street. In 1925, at a cost of $4,000, the congregation voted to build a

tabernacle which was used for worship services for 25 years.

At the close of World War II, Trinity's membership began raising funds for a new Sanctuary. The church itself served as general contractor for the building, which was designed by Louis Gamble. Members of the congregation volunteered more than 6,000 man hours to build the Sanctuary, working Saturdays and whenever possible during the week. Every Saturday for two years, ladies of the church served lunch to the workers. In November, 1950, the new Sanctuary was dedicated.

Judson Studios executed the stained glass windows, using such recurring Trinity motifs as three pendants hanging from the Star of Regeneration, and three fleur de lis, ancient symbols of the Trinity. Themes of the windows include the writers of the four Gospels, the cross and crown of thorns and the regal crown, attesting to the biblical statement "Thine is the kingdom," the tablets of the law, the heritage of the prophets, symbolized by the harp of the Psalmist and the scroll of Isaiah, and the Lamb and the Cross. The rose window is unusual in its coloration: pinks, lavenders, blue and gold replace the more typical deep blues and reds.

A triptych on the baptistery wall is fashioned in three panels, again reiterating the theme of the Trinity. The dove of the center panel represents the Holy Spirit which descended on Jesus after his baptism. The six-pointed star of David on the left panel symbolizes Jehovah, while the five-pointed star of Epiphany and the Maltese cross of the right panel represent Christian symbolism for Jesus.

FIGHT
THE
GOOD FIGHT

ALL THINGS BRIGHT
AND BEAUTIFUL,
ALL CREATURES
GREAT AND SMALL,
ALL THINGS WISE
AND WONDERFUL
THE LORD, GOD
MADE THEM ALL.

PREACH
THE WORD

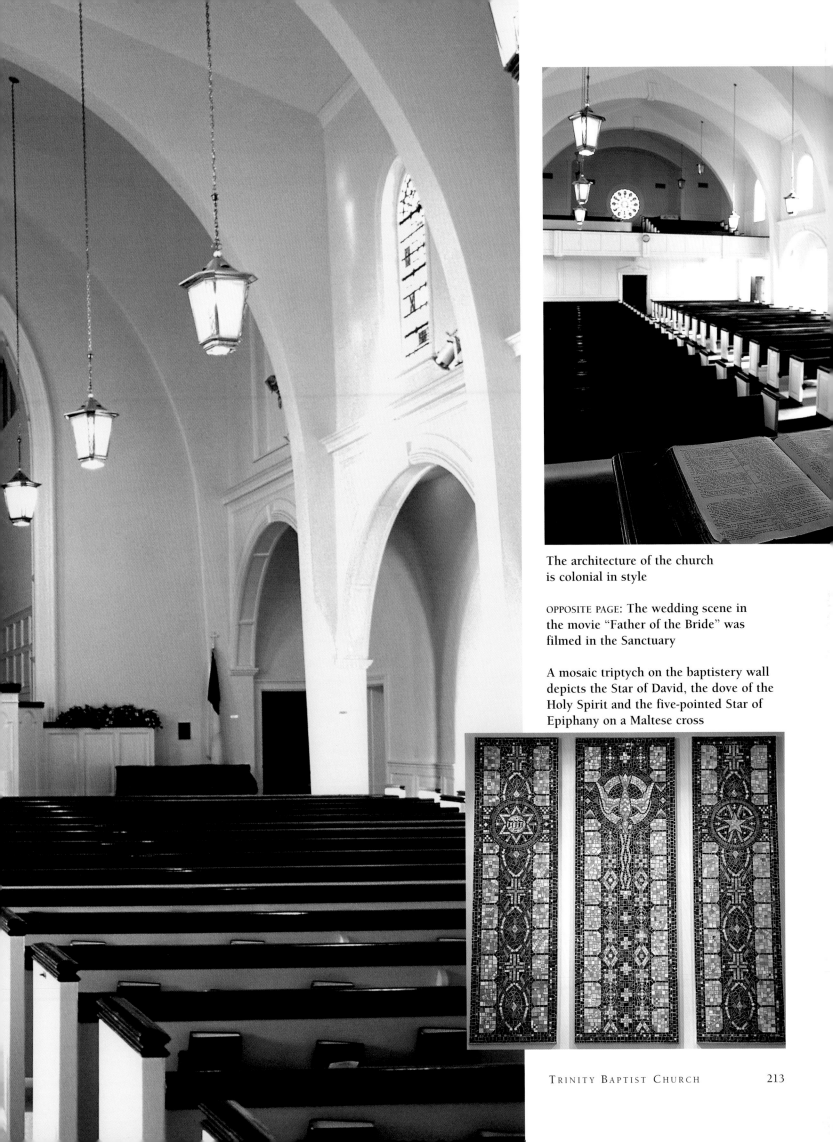

The architecture of the church is colonial in style

OPPOSITE PAGE: The wedding scene in the movie "Father of the Bride" was filmed in the Sanctuary

A mosaic triptych on the baptistery wall depicts the Star of David, the dove of the Holy Spirit and the five-pointed Star of Epiphany on a Maltese cross

UNIVERSITY OF SOUTHERN CALIFORNIA
LITTLE CHAPEL OF SILENCE

Adjacent to the Town and Gown building at the University of Southern California is the 30-seat capacity Little Chapel of Silence. Donated to the school in 1935 by Mrs. Walter Harrison Fisher, a member of the university's board of trustees, it provides students with a quiet place for prayer and meditation. Weddings are held here, as well as services by various campus religious organizations.

Stained glass is used as an inset in the door, and as round windows in the chapel walls

Little Chapel of Silence, Los Angeles

The entrance with a quatrefoil window

OPPOSITE PAGE: Although a favorite place for weddings, the chapel was designed to inspire meditation in the midst of academia.

FAR RIGHT: Painted ceiling beams

214

UNIVERSITY OF SOUTHERN CALIFORNIA
UNITED UNIVERSITY CHURCH

United University Church, Los Angeles

RIGHT: **An early name plaque**

OPPOSITE PAGE: **The colonnade of modified Corinthian columns**

Details of the exterior stonework

Although the initial gifts of land for the original campus of University of Southern California were donated by a Catholic, a Protestant and a Jew, it was the Methodist Church which officially opened USC in 1880. For more than 70 years the Methodist connection to the university continued: the early football team was nicknamed "The Fighting Methodists," and until 1928 the USC board of trustees was selected by the Conference of the Methodist Church.

Not surprisingly, University Methodist Church was founded in 1881, less than a year after USC itself. The church's first building was at Wesley Avenue and Simpson Street, where the Student Union now stands. A second church was constructed at McClintock and West Jefferson streets, and in 1931, the current Italian Romanesque building was dedicated. The architect was Raimond Johnson, a member of the church board who was also on the faculty of the USC School of Architecture.

In 1965, University Methodist invited First Presbyterian Church to share its building. Today, United University belongs to both the Presbyterian and the United Methodist churches, with full standing in both denominations.

delicate capital of one of
olumns that line the sides
e church

The church was designed
by Raimond Johnson,
who taught architecture
at USC

A lantern illumines the
stonework at the back
wall of the church

RIGHT: The window
dedicated to St. Barbara

The rose window

Lanterns illumine the
wood ceiling beams

The ship is an early
symbol of the
Christian church

WARD AFRICAN METHODIST EPISCOPAL CHURCH

Ward African Methodist Episcopal Church,
Los Angeles

RIGHT: **The baptismal font**

OPPOSITE PAGE: **The church's musical
section, complementing the organ**

A panel of stained glass

Originally known as the Los
Angeles Mission, Ward A.M.E. Church
began in 1902 with services held in a
private home. Several subsequent
moves and name changes later, the
church united with the California
Conference of the African Methodist
Episcopal Church in 1910. In 1914 the
church chose the name Ward Chapel to
honor its minister Rev. Milton Ward,
and in 1937, with a membership of
more than 1200, the congregation
became known as Ward A.M.E.
Church.

In 1951 the congregation
purchased its current home, a former
Lutheran church which can seat 600
worshippers
in its blue
and gold
Sanctuary.
Trimmed with
Gothic-style
woodwork,
the Sanctuary
is illumined
by pastel
stained glass
windows. In
the Italian
tradition, the
ceiling is
painted to
resemble a blue sky with wispy clouds,
and a galaxy of electric pin spot lights
completes the charming effect.

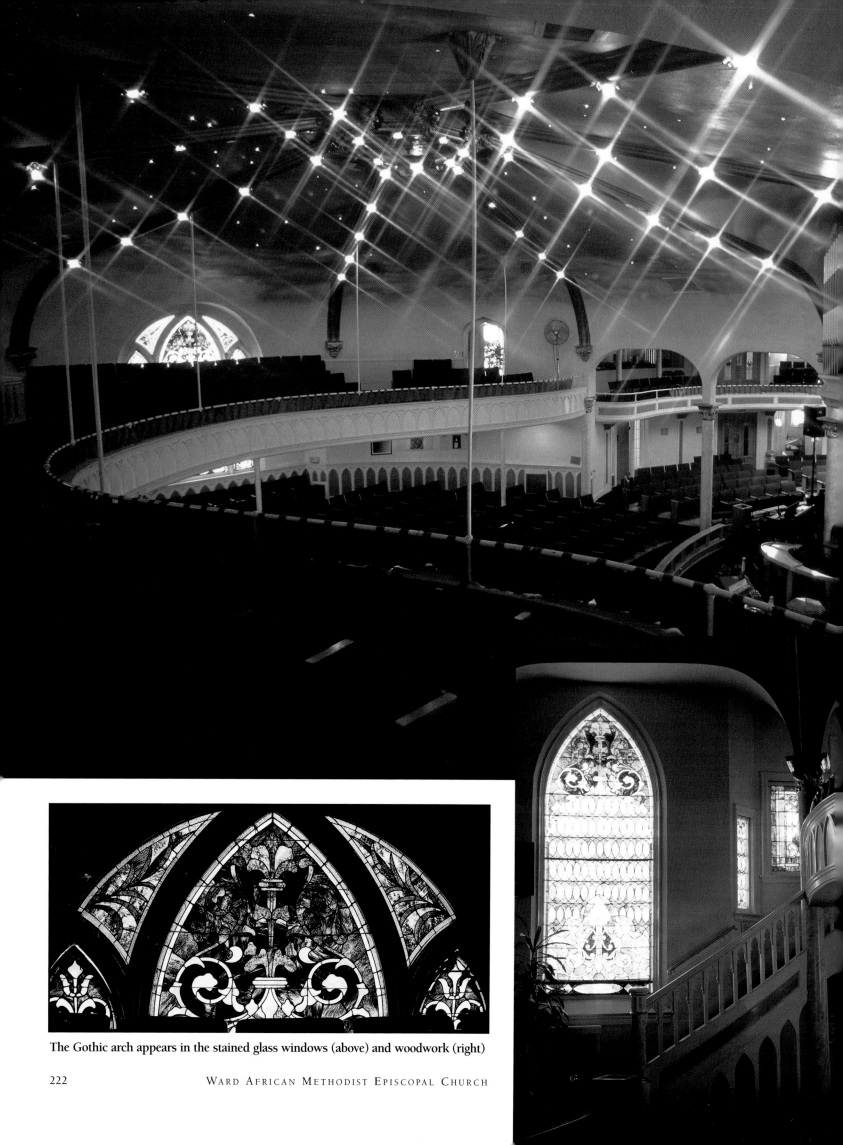

The Gothic arch appears in the stained glass windows (above) and woodwork (right)

The organ pipes

The altar

When the Sanctuary is darkened, the sky-painted ceiling twinkles

The windows of the balcony

The colorful dome at the far side of the Sanctuary

WILSHIRE CHRISTIAN CHURCH

Wilshire Christian Church, Los Angeles

RIGHT: An ornate capital of a balcony column

OPPOSITE PAGE: Each spoke of the rose window includes symbols of the names and titles of Jesus, such as "The bright morning star"

Lacy grill work in the chancel

The first recorded meeting of the Disciples of Christ denomination in Los Angeles was a Breaking of Bread service in the County Court house in August, 1874. The first church was organized downtown the next year. By 1910, the developing Wilshire Center area was the focus of the outreach of the Disciples of Christ's Wilshire Boulevard Christian Church. Services were originally held in a rented home on S. Normandie Avenue, and when the congregation outgrew the space, it purchased an enormous tent, put down a wooden floor, furnished it appropriately for a church, and proceeded to conduct services, to the delight of the contemporary media.

A gift of property at Wilshire Boulevard and Normandie Avenue from the three Chapman brothers, who owned a hotel in the area as well as the Chapman Marketplace on Sixth Street, ensured the church an ongoing home in the area. The church purchased an adjacent lot on which to built "the Bungalow," a temporary home, which met its needs until the early 1920s, when a building campaign began for a permanent new edifice at Wilshire Boulevard and Normandie Avenue.

Architect Robert H. Orr designed an Italian Romanesque structure of reinforced concrete, completing it in 1923. Over five of the exterior doorways are bas-relief reproductions of Old Master paintings of events in the life of Christ. The massive stained glass rose window, a copy of the one in Rheims Cathedral, was designed by Judson Studios. The hammered copper cross over the pulpit was made by a member of the church. The overhead roof beams which appear to be wood are in fact structural steel, covered in plaster and painted to look like wood.

By 1940, two other Disciples of Christ congregations had merged with Wilshire Boulevard Christian, and the name was changed to Wilshire Christian Church.

To build and furnish the entire church in 1927 cost just over $400,000.

LEFT: The delicate balcony railing

Concrete grill work above the balcony

A stenciled roof beam

OPPOSITE PAGE: The baptistery at Wilshire Christian is located behind the pulpit

WILSHIRE CHRISTIAN CHURCH

227

WILSHIRE UNITED METHODIST CHURCH

Wilshire United Methodist Church

RIGHT: One of the church's two rose windows

OPPOSITE PAGE: Stained glass windows commemorate Fr. Junipero Serra, as well as the teachings of Jesus

A window of roses

The congregation which built what is now Wilshire United Methodist Church was inspired by its location at Plymouth and Wilshire boulevards. The cast stone structure was built in 1924 by the firm Allison and Allison for the All Souls' Congregational Church, which honored its Pilgrim heritage – and its Plymouth, England connection – in architectural details throughout the building. Over the entry to the central door is an illustration of the signing of the Civil Compact aboard the Mayflower. In the Sanctuary, the civic pulpit on the left of the podium is emblazoned with the coat of arms of Governor Bradford of the Plymouth Colony, and the preaching pulpit carries the coat of arms of Elder Brewster, who led the Pilgrims to the shores of the New World.

The Wilshire United Methodist congregation began in 1887 as the Simpson Methodist Episcopal Church. Merging with several other Methodist congregations over the years, in 1931 the membership purchased its current building from All Souls' Congregational. The church has always been an extremely popular site for weddings; Shirley Temple married her first husband, actor John Agar, here, and in 1937, singing star Jeanette MacDonald wed Gene Raymond in a ceremony which columnist Louella O. Parsons described as "Reverently beautiful as a picture from a medieval princess story book…. Outside were more than 10,000 loyal well-wishers and fans, who gathered to call friendly greetings to the stars who were invited, and to cheer the bridal party."

For many years, Wilshire United Methodist sponsored an annual Madonna Festival, to which artists were invited to submit paintings, mosaics or sculptures on the subject "Motherhood in Art." Although the competition is no longer held, many of the artworks have been installed in the entry to the church.

In 1994, an arson fire, which started in the organ loft, devastated most of the original Sanctuary of the church. Restoration has been exact, including the intricate re-stenciling of the paneled wooden ceiling, which alone required 10,000 hours to complete.

The Memory
of Him
Shall not
Depart Away

To John Steven McGroarty

Who has rekindled in California
our devotion to Junipero Serra

Wrought iron gates to a chapel where
weddings are often held

The nave is 164 feet long,
60 feet wide and seats 1400.

Detail of ceiling
stenciling

INDEX

All Saints' Episcopal Church
504 North Camden Drive
Beverly Hills, CA 90210
310 275 0123
www.allsaintsbh.org

All Saints Episcopal Church
132 North Euclid Avenue
Pasadena, CA 91101-1796
626 796 1172
www.allsaints-pas.org

Cathedral of Our Lady of the Angels
555 West Temple Street
Los Angeles, CA 90012-2707
213 680 5200
www.olacathedral.org

Christ the King Roman Catholic Church
624 North Rossmore Avenue
Los Angeles, CA 90004
323 465 7605
www.ctk-la.org

Church of St. Charles Borromeo
10828 Moorpark Street
North Hollywood, CA 91602-2206
818 766 3838

Church of the Angels
1100 Avenue 64
Pasadena, CA 91505
323 255 3878
www.thechurchoftheangels.org

Church of the Blessed Sacrament
6657 Sunset Boulevard
Los Angeles, CA 90028
323 462 6311
www.blessedsacramenthollywood.org

Church of the Good Shepherd
505 North Bedford Drive
Beverly Hills, CA 90210
310 285 5425
www.shepherd.catholicweb.com

First African Methodist Episcopal Church
2270 South Harvard Street
Los Angeles, CA 90018
323 730 9180
www.famechurch@famechurch.org

First Baptist Church
760 South Westmoreland Avenue
Los Angeles, CA 90005
213 384 2151
www.firstbaptistla.org

First United Methodist Church
of North Hollywood
4832 Tujunga Avenue
North Hollywood, CA 91601
818 763 8231
www.nohomethodistchurch.com

Good Shepherd Center
for Homeless Women
        Irene Wierman Chapel
650 Rockwood Street
Los Angeles, CA 90026
213 482 1834
www.thegoodshepherdcenter.com

First Congregational Church
of Los Angeles
540 South Commonwealth Avenue
Los Angeles, CA 90020
213 385 1341
www.fccla.org

First United Methodist Church
of Pasadena
500 East Colorado Boulevard
Pasadena, CA 91101
626 796 0157
www.fumcpasadena.org

Holy Family Catholic Church
1501 Fremont Avenue
South Pasadena, CA 91030
626 799 8908
www.holyfamily.org

First Presbyterian Church of Hollywood
1760 North Gower Street
Los Angeles, CA 90028
323 463 7161
www.fpch.org

Good Samaritan Hospital
        All Souls Chapel
616 South Witmer Street
Los Angeles, CA 90017
213 977 2121

Holy Virgin Mary Russian
Orthodox Cathedral
650 Micheltorena Street
Los Angeles, CA 90026
323 666 4977
www.hvmecathedral.org

Immanuel Presbyterian Church
3300 Wilshire Boulevard
Los Angeles, CA 90010
213 389 3191
www.Immanuelpres.org

Loyola Marymount University
    Sacred Heart Chapel
    Huesman Chapel
    The Jesuit Community Chapel
One LMU Drive
Los Angeles, CA 90045-2659
310 338 2700
www.lmu.edu

Pepperdine University
    Stauffer Chapel
24255 Pacific Coast Highway
Malibu, CA 90263
310 506 4000
www.pepperdine.edu

St. Alban's Episcopal Church
580 Hilgard Avenue
Westwood, CA 90024
310 208 6516
www.stalbanswestwood.com

St. Andrew Catholic Church
311 North Raymond Avenue
Pasadena, CA 91103
626 792 4183
www.standrewpasadena.org

St. Brendan Catholic Church
310 South Van Ness Avenue
Los Angeles, CA 90020
323 936 4656
www.stbrendanchurch.org

St. James' Episcopal Church
3903 Wilshire Boulevard
Los Angeles, CA 90010-3212
213 388 3417
www.saintjamesla.org

St. John's Episcopal Church
514 West Adams Boulevard
Los Angeles, CA 90007
213 747 6285
www.stjohnsla.org

St. Mark's Episcopal Church
1020 North Brand Boulevard
Glendale, CA 91202
818 240 3860
www.saintmarksglendale.com

St. Mary of the Angels Anglican Church
4510 Finley Avenue
Hollywood, CA 90027
323 660 2700

St. Matthew's
(The Parish of St. Matthew's)
1031 Bienveneda Avenue
Pacific Palisades, CA 90272
310 454 1358
www.stmatthews.com

St. Monica Catholic Church
701 California Avenue
Santa Monica, CA 90403-4097
310 393 9287
www.stmonica.net

St. Nicholas Antiochian
Orthodox Cathedral
2300 West Third Street
Los Angeles, CA 90057
213 382 6269
www.stnicholasla.com

St. Timothy Catholic Church
10425 West Pico Boulevard
Los Angeles, CA 90064
310 474 1216
www.sttimothyla.org

St. Vincent de Paul
Catholic Church
621 West Adams Boulevard
Los Angeles, CA 90007
213 749 8950
www.stvincentla.org

The Cathedral Center of St. Paul
840 Echo Park Avenue
Los Angeles, CA 90026
213 482 2040
www.ladiocese.org

University of Southern California
Little Chapel of Silence
3551 University Avenue
Los Angeles, CA 90089
213 740 2311
www.usc.edu

Wilshire Christian Church
634 South Normandie Avenue
Los Angeles, CA 90005
213 382 6337
www.wchrisla.org

The Cathedral of St. Sophia
1324 South Normandie Avenue
Los Angeles, CA 90006
213 737 2424
www.stsophia.org

University of Southern California
United University Church
817 West 34th Street
Los Angeles, CA 90007-3502
213 740 0209

Wilshire United Methodist Church
711 South Plymouth Boulevard
Los Angeles, CA 90005
323 931 1085

Trinity Baptist Church
1015 California Avenue
Santa Monica, CA 90403-4198
310 395 9961
www.trinitysantamonica.com

Ward African Methodist Episcopal Church
1177 West 25th Street
Los Angeles, CA 90007
213 747 1367
www.wardame.org

GLOSSARY

Ambulatory: A covered hall or aisle on the sides of the nave.

Apse: Usually a domed part of the church that projects out behind the altar or at the East end of the church.

Baldachino: A decorative canopy often of stone or marble over the altar of a church.

Baptistery: A part of a church used for baptizing. A separate area, room, pool, building or font.

Basilica: Building oblong in shape with semicircular apse at one end.

Cathedra: Official chair of a Bishop.

Clerestory: Area high above the sides of the sanctuary leading to the altar usually with stained glass windows. Can be above the ambulatory.

Chancel: Area around the altar sometimes enclosed.

Columbarium Chapel: A repository for the ashes of cremated parishioners.

Cruciform: Cross like in form. A term used to define the design of a nave of a church.

Della Robbia: A style of sculpting and ceramics of glazed terra cotta created by the Florentine family, Ghiberti and Nanni di Banco, during the 14th and 15th centuries.

Epiphany: Christian festival, January 6, celebrating the manifestation of the divine nature of Christ to the Gentiles represented by the Magi.

Epistolarin: Written in the form of the letters as written in the New Testament of the Bible.

Evangelist: Usually refers to the New Testament Evangelists Matthew, Mark, Luke and John.

Icon: An image or representation of a religious figure.

Iconostasion: Screen dividing the sanctuary from the main body of the church in an Eastern Orthodox church.

Jesse Tree: Reference to Isaiah 11:1, "A shoot will spring forth from the stump of Jesse, and a branch out of his roots." A tree used during the Advent Season adorned with religious symbols.

Lectern: A slanted raised area or platform where scripture is read during services. Usually smaller than the pulpit.

Magi: (magus singular) The three wise men in Bethlehem.

Magnificat: Canticle (chant or song) praising the Lord.

Narthex: Entry area leading to the nave of a church. A lobby of an early Christian or Byzantine church or basilica.

Nave: The central part of the church sanctuary leading from the narthex (entry lobby) to the alter chancel area with aisles on each side.

Pulpit: Raised area or platform where sermons and announcements are given.

Quatrefoil: A representation of a flower or leaf with four petals or leaves used in the art of designing genealogies and coats of arms. Used to rule on the questions of rank or protocol, usually in heraldry or pageantry. It is also used in church symbolism to represent the four gospels and four evangelists.

Relic: An object of religious veneration, especially an article or remains, associated with a saint or martyr. These are usually kept in a special area of a sanctuary.

Reredos: The wall behind the alter, usually decorated, painted or with stained glass window.

Rood cross: Medieval English term for the beam across the chancel of a church.

Rose Window: A symbol of eternity. Usually placed at either end of the nave, but can be at both ends. Also placed in transept walls. Named the rose because it is shaped like a rose. Small circles and color create the style of most rose windows however tracery bars in radiating order is another design often used.

Tabernacle: Place where the Holy Host is kept. Usually in a locked box of metal. Sometimes kept in the sanctuary or put in away until Communion is served. It can be a sacred portable sanctuary (tent) as the nomads used in the First Testament.

Te Deum window: Te Deum is a format for praise, a hymn or window.

Transept: When a church is built in cruciform design, cross form, the transept is either of the two arms of the cross.

Transfiguration: The sudden radiance from Jesus on the mountain with Peter, James and John where Elijah and Moses appeared to them and God spoke. Christians celebrate this observance on August 6.

Trefoil: Representing the Holy Trinity. Vine, leaves, grapes reference to Christ.

Triptych: Painting or carving with three hinged panels, usually religious in design.

Vestibule: A small entrance hall.

Acknowledgements

This dream would not have come true without the support of these and more.

To the churches:

A special thank you to every church that opened their doors to us and "turned on the lights." And to each staff member who went the extra mile and dug deep to find the answers to all the questions that made this book historically correct.

To the friends for the hand holding, prayers and opening of doors:

Jane Ackerman, Linda Adams, Rev. Carol Anderson, Rev. Betsy Anderson, Vera Babb, Shirley and Julian Capata, Timi Loomis Freshman, Jane Galbraith, Jane Gilman, Kathy Gless, Joyce Haight, Terry and Ben Hayes, Phyllis Hennigan, Sonia Hernandez, Betsy and Clyde Jackson, Jimmy Karatsikis, Councilman Tom La Bonge, Linda Leich, Georgia and Tom Lile, Sandra Mansour, Bonnie McClure, Dede and John McNicholas, Claudia Polley, Colm Ryle, Jeanette Webster

To Family for all the advice, editing, indulgence, budgets and phone calls made:

Bruce, my husband and partner, Sondra and Wayne Jones, Pamela Ludwig, Don Ludwig, Marguerite Ludwig, Charla Ludwig Thompson, Ryan Thompson, Brianne and Randy Sanada, Suzanne and Paul Wierman for the gift of Brianne, Pamela and George Wurzel

For the Mentors around the world who gave me inspiration and courage:

Carol Beckwith and Angela Fisher, David Coulson, Lady Mavis Coulson, Mary Cross, Dr. Zahi Hawas, Dr. Donald Johanson, Dr. Mark Lehner, Mark Lenz, Cynthia Moss, Gayle Roski, Dr. Kent Weeks, Don Young

To those who made all the production come through:

Somehow everyone involved became a team, remarking that they loved this project. I believe we were meant to meet.

Design, Morris Jackson
Photography, Brianne Sanada
Text, Sydney Swire

Paper Chase Printing, Inc.:
Richard Restler, Aaron Katz and Chris Milos
Marina Rosales, Manny Rosales, Roman Faiman, Chuck Haydel, Fernando Ortiz, Nicole Katz, Sofia Chavez, Ron Bennett, Dario Sanchez, Jerry Galvan, Jesus Barrera, Jesus Flores, Angelica Rosales, Ever Morris, Harry Green, Mila Salas

Larchmont Photo:
Bob Niemerow

West Coast Photo:
Khristina Kerseles and Pam Lent

Proceeds from Jewels in Our Crown benefit homeless women and children served by the Sisters of the Lovers of the Holy Cross, the St. Joseph Sisters of Carondelet with Sister Julia Mary at Good Shepherd Center for Homeless Women.

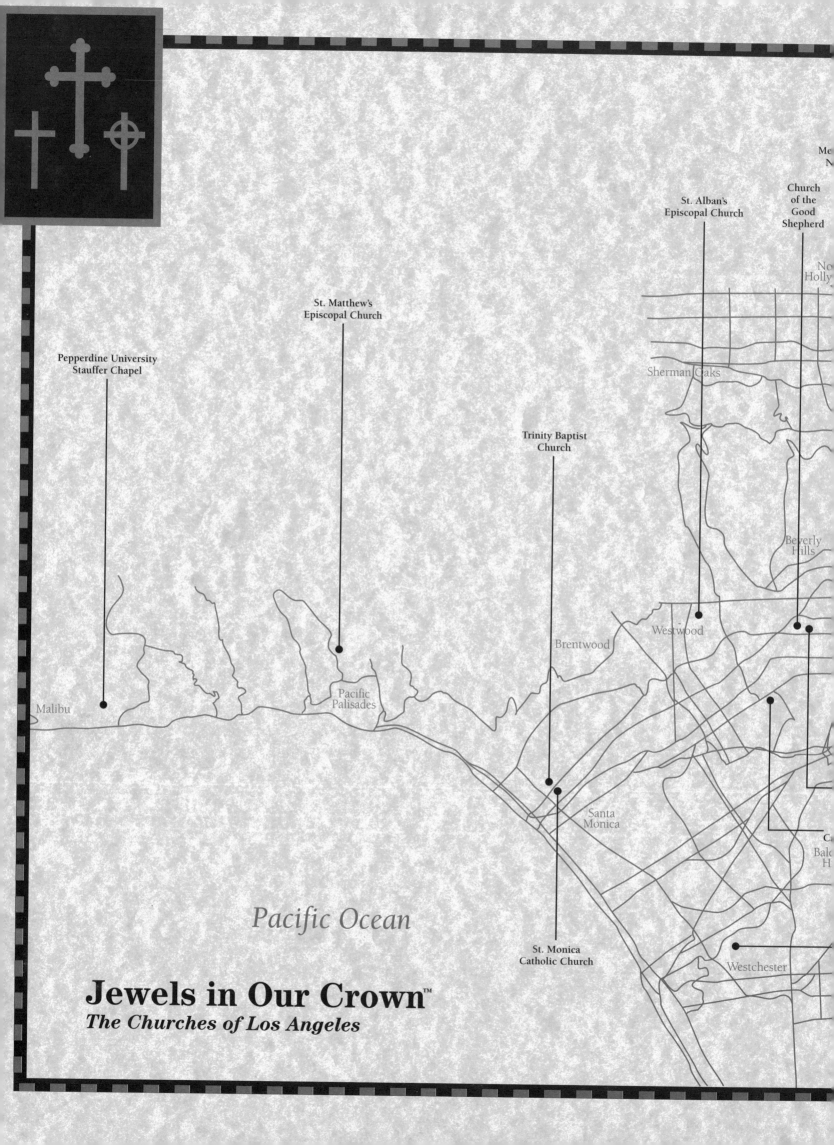

Me
N

Church
of the
Good
Shepherd

St. Alban's
Episcopal Church

No
Holly

St. Matthew's
Episcopal Church

Sherman Oaks

Pepperdine University
Stauffer Chapel

Beverly
Hills

Trinity Baptist
Church

Westwood

Brentwood

Malibu

Pacific
Palisades

Ca
Balc
H

Santa
Monica

Pacific Ocean

St. Monica
Catholic Church

Westchester

Jewels in Our Crown™
The Churches of Los Angeles